From A Parent's Perspective

Janet Gonzalez-Mena

Sheffield Publishing Company

Salem, Wisconsin

For information about this book, write or call:
Sheffield Publishing Company
P.O. Box 359
Salem, Wisconsin 53168
(414) 843-2281

Dedication

To my children, Bruce, Bret, Robin, Adam, and Tim

Acknowledgements

I thank:

Tad Parker who has been incredibly helpful and supportive.

The Ariadne Writers Group of the Napa Valley, who give me loving feedback: Lin Rogers, Pam Burns-Clair, Catherine Romberg-Bump, Betsy Allbright, Jean Boyce-Smith, Marilyn Landeros, Sharon Silver, Elizabeth Harris, and Sharon Elwell.

Doug Ernst, who gave me a start as a newspaper columnist. Doug is Managing Editor of the *Napa Valley Register* where these articles first appeared.

Sandra Drake, who encouraged me to turn the columns into a book and then tirelessly marketed the self-published edition as a fundraiser for the Napa Valley College Child Care Center.

Royalties from the sale of this book go to benefit the Napa Valley College Child Care Center.

Foreword

Parents need a lot of support to be successful. Those who were wise or lucky enough to take some courses in child development or parenting are the exceptions to the rule. Even then, the theory does not always prepare one for the reality. Ask any parent who has been up three nights straight with a screaming infant.

Thank goodness, every once in a while, a writer like Janet Gonzalez-Mena comes along to help lift the heavy burden of parenthood with her compassion, humanity, and not least of all, **humor**. Janet is an accomplished educator, researcher and author in the fields of child development and early childhood education. She is also a mother of five, well-seasoned by practice as well as theory.

Janet's series of articles, compiled in this book, beautifully bridges the gap between high-flown educational theories, and the nitty-gritty, everyday problems all parents must deal with. In every chapter you will find a new and surprising point of view that will stretch your perception of how things can be done.

Janet's message is to be gentle with your child and with yourself, learn from your mistakes and never be afraid to say, "I'm sorry" even to yourself. Janet's perspective encourages parents to be flexible, observant, and not too attached to expectations. Children are individuals and will become themselves. We, as parents, cannot control that process—nor should we try.

If you are a parent, have had a parent, or are planning to become a parent, or work with parents in the future, you will come away from Janet's writing more relaxed, more tolerant, and chuckling to yourself. That's just what we parents need!

Beverly J. Aguilar, M.Ed.
Director, Napa Valley College Child-Family Center

CONTENTS

Introduction

I've been teaching parenting classes for twenty-five years. Every semester, at least one student tells me that he or she is taking the course to "learn how to do it right." Well, I've got some news—there is no right way to parent!

There are no absolutes in parenting—no formulas, no rights or wrongs—only an array of outcomes. Here's more news—much as we may want to, we can't control the outcomes.

Control is a big issue in parenting. I learned a long time ago that the harder I try to take control, the more likely I am to lose it. It would be nice to be able to say, "I'll do this, this, and this; and my child will turn out just the way I want." It just doesn't work that way. The good news is we can't blame ourselves for what we perceive as our failures. The bad news is we can't congratulate ourselves for what we consider successes either.

Parenting is a **human** endeavor. When parents become too concerned about parenting "correctly" they can be afflicted with a condition known as "analysis paralysis." Because they are so worried about doing everything just right, when faced with a decision, they get stuck. They can't act. Analysis paralysis can be a big problem!

Luckily, as a parent, I was seldom afflicted with this condition. Not being a perfectionist, I just bungled ahead. Some of the stories about my bungling are contained in this volume. My words of advice are part of those stories, as well as issues to think about and discuss.

I

SURVIVING PARENTHOOD

Take care of yourself *and* your child;
you'll be a better parent if you're
fulfilled and satisfied.

Photo credit: Jim Darter

DON'T GET INVESTED IN CONFLICT

"Watch that sailboat," my husband told me pointing out a sloop off-shore from where we were anchored on our vacation in the San Juan Islands right by the Washington-Canadian border.

"That boat isn't making any more progress than we are," he said.

I didn't believe it. There was wind; in fact, the boat was heeling, which indicated a strong wind. But as the day went on, that boat never moved. It stayed just off the point where we first noticed it. It was sailing, yet standing still.

"I wonder when they will notice they haven't made any headway," my husband said. "They think they are sailing right along. The water roaring by the hull and the wind whistling in the sails is making enough commotion to fool them into believing that they're making progress—it's just that they're not moving forward."

"Why not?" I asked.

"They're bucking the tide. They're sailing through the water but not over the ground. The current is too strong."

Suddenly, I realized that same situation applies to parenting and indeed to all human relationships. I think of times I've been in conflict with someone; one of my children, my husband, my sister, or even someone I work with. The roar and commotion of the conflict makes me feel as if forward progress is being made. I am moving through the water. I watch it flow around the sides of the hull and leave a foamy wake behind. I can hear and feel the wind. I'm sailing but not making any progress. When I finally take a bearing to discover where I am, I find myself in exactly the spot where I started.

In a boat, once you discover you aren't moving, you have several options:

- You can choose to keep right on sailing and enjoy it even without making progress.

- If you have a goal in mind, you can try trimming your sails to increase your speed and change your course enough to get out of the strongest current.

- If you aren't goal-oriented, you can turn around and go the other way—**with** the tide instead of against it.

That's all true of me in a conflict too. Once I manage to wake up to what's happening, I can make the same kinds of decisions.

I can decide if I want to continue with the roar and commotion and not worry about getting anywhere. I have discovered more than once that all the fuss was serving some purpose. The conflict wasn't about resolution but about roar and commotion. I was more invested in fighting than I was in finding solutions. In fact, some of my relationships seem to be centered around turmoil—especially the one with my daughter.

I also have the option to change course or trim my sails. That is, I can try something different to resolve the conflict or at least make progress.

I can even turn around and sail the other way leaving the conflict entirely. It takes two to fight. If one leaves, the other doesn't have anybody to fight with. I don't have to physically leave the scene, I can just stop fighting.

I have another option too. I can anchor and just watch the current flow by while waiting for more favorable conditions—a stronger wind or the turn of the tide.

Effective conflict resolution is often just a matter of timing. Sometimes I forget that fact when I'm bucking some tide or getting swept into a flow I didn't choose. Timing is everything when you're dealing with strong forces. It's better to work with them than against them.

The important thing is to recognize what's actually happening and to realize that you have a choice about how to respond to the situation.

It seems to me that's good advice for parents, for partners, for anyone who is in a relationship that involves conflict. It's also good advice for sailors.

2

BALANCING NEEDS

Getting needs met is the answer to healthy growth, long life, satisfaction, and self esteem—for both you and your child. Yet nothing is more difficult than meeting your child's needs and your own at the same time. Parents must be constantly juggling, trying to keep all these various needs from colliding.

Not only do you have to be a juggler but you have to be an interpreter as well. Understanding who needs what is vital. Sometimes parents have trouble distinguishing their own needs from those of their children. For example, it's the middle of the night. You're anxious and you can't sleep. Your sleeping baby whimpers in the other room. You go in and pick him up and carry him to your bed telling yourself that he's unhappy and needs comforting. Are your own needs influencing your reading of his?

Another example—you were a child who grew up in hand-me-down clothes, so you buy your daughter one expensive dress after another. Is that what **she** needs?

It is important that we distinguish our own wants and needs from those of our children.

What happens when you've read the needs right but they conflict with your own? Then you have to make decisions and establish priorities. For example, your toddler is still asleep but you have to wake her up so you can get to work on time. Or you're finally inspired to work on the article you've promised to write for your organization's newsletter, when your daughter comes begging you to take her to the park. Can you say no and still feel okay?

Children are resilient. They can cope with their needs being put second sometimes—as long as their needs aren't **always** second in your priorities.

Parents can get so busy taking care of their children that they neglect taking care of themselves. Yet getting your own needs met is the key to meeting those of your children. You can't always put yourself last and end up strong, healthy, and able to meet the incredible challenges of parenting.

So how can you manage to meet your needs and still do your job as a parent? Just like juggling, it takes both skill and motivation to learn. Here are some tips:

• **Take care of your physical self.** Eat nourishing food. Give your body attention on a regular basis. Do what you need to focus on your body and its health. (A massage? A long bath? A workout?) Find ways to get both regular exercise and enough rest.

• **Take care of your emotional and social self.** You need support. Get it! If you have a supportive partner, great. But look beyond that one person. Some parents use their extended family for support, others use friends. If support isn't automatically a part of your life—seek it out. You deserve it!

• **Take care of your intellectual self.** This may be the most difficult task of all. By the time you've taken care of your children, your body, and your feelings, you've got no time or energy left for your mind. With family demands pressuring you, intellectual pursuits may seem out of the question. One intellectual task that is always with you is **problem-solving.** You can congratulate yourself on using your head as you deal with child-rearing. Though not always recognized as such, it's a real intellectual task getting everyone's needs met, solving the problems, setting up a safe, yet interesting and challenging environment for your children. And remember, you're doing all this on top of your ordinary living and work chores! But you may have intellectual needs beyond these. Can you find ways to meet them?

Take care of yourself **while** taking care of your children. Recognize your needs and find ways to fulfill them. You'll be a better parent if you're fulfilled and satisfied, at least some of the time!

3

ENDURING ARGUMENTS

When children argue, they're learning
about the give and take of family relationships.

Photo credit: Robin Wallach

Ever get tired of constant squabbling? Sometimes it seems as if that's all kids do—argue and bicker over every little thing. It's enough to drive a parent crazy.

After living with this situation for years, here's my considered advice about it.

Don't stop kids from arguing—only if they threaten each other with physical violence. When they argue they're learning about the give and take of family relationships. These lessons will serve them well as they become involved in close relationships in their adult lives.

Instead of keeping your children from fighting, look for ways to make their squabbles healthier, more effective, and less annoying to you. Here are some suggestions:

- Teach your children arguing skills. Do this through "sports announcing" while an argument is going on. Don't take sides, just help both children verbalize their own points of view and also help them hear each other. Restate their words to each other. "It sounds like you're really mad because she used your brush. Tell her how you feel about that." Don't give your own opinion or take your own stand during this process or you will enter their argument and change it. The learning won't be the same if that happens. Unless the argument has to do with you, you don't belong in it except as a sideline observer.

- Teach your children to fight fair. Don't let them hurt each other. I feel very strongly about no physical violence in my household and, when it seems eminent, I step in. I also feel strongly about verbal violence. I don't mean that feelings won't get hurt as tempers rise. I do mean that I teach alternatives to name-calling, threats, and scathing criticism. For example, if a child has a history for making cutting remarks, I teach her to express her feelings instead of attacking her opponent.

- Determine which arguments are more for your attention than anything else and take your attention away from them. You don't have to be right there in the middle of every battle, and if you are, your children are probably doing it just to get you there. When I had a bunch of little kids at home all yelling at each other, I got good at determining when I was needed to stop violence (both physical and verbal) and when I wasn't. Since I wasn't good at ignoring an argument my children were putting on for my benefit, I often left the room (whenever I felt reasonably assured that it was safe for me to do so). Sometimes the fighting parties followed me, trying harder and harder to draw me in to their disagreement. I remember times sitting behind the locked bathroom door with the fan on so I couldn't be drawn in no matter what they said to me.

It isn't pleasant living in a house with constant struggle going on. However, it's a lot healthier than living with those same struggles running as strong, silent underground streams, influencing everything that happens but seldom coming out onto the surface to be dealt with openly.

How are children to learn to express feelings and meet needs in conjunction with a peer if they don't fight? How can they solve conflicts and sort out disagreements if they don't engage in regular arguments? Childhood squabbles prepare children for developing close relationships in adulthood. Don't let them drive you crazy.

═══ 4 ═══

PARENTS AS CONNECTORS

I often find myself caught in the middle. I'm either a connector putting two people in touch with each other (like my husband and son) or I'm squeezed between two powerful forces who are in conflict with each other. If you have more than one child, and they fight now and then, you know what I mean.

Here's how I feel when I'm caught in the middle of someone else's conflict: I'm squeezed until I begin to feel my energy, indeed my very brains, under great pressure. Eventually, if I don't get out of the way of the forces in conflict, my energy is squeezed out through my pores and my brains pop right out my ears. Not a pretty picture.

Afterwards, I'm not a pretty picture either—I'm a deflated, human-shaped balloon—used, flat, and full of puckers, wrinkles, and stretch marks. It's a wonder that I ever fill up again and am able to walk and talk in human form with both brains and energy restored.

The problem is that I'm an open-minded person. I'm a good listener; I'm sensitive. I don't know if that came with parenthood or if I was that way before—it's been so long now that I can't remember my life B. C. (before children).

These caught-in-the-middle-times are when the argument isn't mine. I surely have my own issues—things I feel strongly about and areas I want to use my power to change. But I seem to be a magnet for other people's issues also. I often find myself with angry people on either side slugging it out—right through me.

I am a great person to be in the middle because I can usually see both points of view clearly. Although both parties are always wanting me to take sides, I can't seem to let one perception go to the exclusion of the other. I'm on both sides at once, so of course both sides are mad at me as well as at each other.

The challenge for me, and for any of you who find yourself in this position, is to be a listening, reflecting, understanding, sensitive person and protect yourself at the same time.

Sometimes I can do this juggling act. It takes awareness and presence of mind to do that. I have to be conscious of what is happening. I have to separate my issues and my feelings from those of the arguing parties.

The best way to describe how I do this is to say I step back. Two of my children will be telling me their differing stories. I leave my body there in the middle and take my awareness off to one side. It's like being in a picture hanging on a wall. You can't see the picture until you step out of it. Once I am sufficiently removed, I can watch what is happening while directing my body, mind, and feelings from this new vantage point.

When I do this well, I can keep the conflicting forces off myself, thereby holding my own energy inside and preventing my brains from popping out. I can also avoid exploding, which is a definite threat when explosive energy is pounding on me and the sparks are flying.

It isn't just these dramatic moments that are the problem; it's also being in the middle of the little daily interactions that empties me.

Someone once said that being a parent is like being an old-fashioned telephone switchboard operator. That image really struck home. I can just see the operator sporting earphone and mouthpiece, confronted by a spaghetti tangle of wires and a board filled with holes to plug them into. At home with my family, I often sit in the operator's chair with every single call going right through me. I'm a connector. "Mom, ask Dad if he'll pick me up today." "Tell Robin that I want a ride to the store." "How come Timmy left his socks on my computer?"

When I'm doing a good job I can send the calls on without any drain on my own energy. But that takes time and sometimes I can't prevent the drain. I have solved the problem, though. I discovered a while back that I can teach each member of my family **direct dialing**. Oh, it's a modern world we live in!

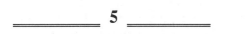

5

A STRENGTH CAN BE A WEAKNESS

Powers of concentration can make you a
"space case" *or* help you focus on your child.
Photo credit: Jim Darter

"They should have named you Oblivia," my husband said to me.

"Huh?" I answered without looking up from my book.

"You didn't even hear me," he accused.

"Sure I did—Oblivia..." my eyes continued to move across the page.

"See what I mean?" My husband gave up and went back to his computer—his own way of reaching the Land of Oblivion.

My husband is right—sometimes I'm a space case. It's one of my greatest strengths and also one of my greatest weaknesses.

My powers of concentration are well-developed. That's how I got through the noise and bustle of a college dorm and still managed to study. It's how, as the mother of five children, I have managed to read some books and even write some. Yes, my powers of concentration have served me well.

But, as a parent, my tendency to leave the room without removing my body is a problem that I haven't completely solved. The trick is to be appropriately responsive—as I wasn't with my husband. You need to be able to come in and out of oblivion with ease. It's a vital trick to learn and one I'm still working on.

Granted, children don't need your full attention every moment you are with them. But it's easy for space travel to become a habit so children feel ignored or they know they have to do something fairly drastic to get your attention. (And children are pretty good at thinking up "fairly drastic" actions.)

If you too, like me, should have been named Oblivia, don't despair...and don't kick yourself. It's a healthy defense—it's the way we keep sane. The goal is not to get rid of your powers of concentration but learning to focus them on your children more often. It's good mental discipline to learn to change the focal point of your concentration and it benefits everyone.

What I'm talking about is spending time in the present—in the here and now—with a child. The first step is to become aware of when you are actually doing that. When are you fully present with all your body, senses, feelings and mind? Perhaps not very often. Many of us learned early to separate our body, mind, and feelings. We also learned to live mostly in the past or the future without experiencing very much of the present. If you're one of those people, I urge you to give the present a try—it's quite an experience. And don't do it alone—bring a child along with you.

6

PRESERVING YOUR INDIVIDUALITY

Parenting is a balancing act between getting totally wrapped up in the life of another person and standing apart—remaining a separate individual. To be a parent you have to be able to do both. You have to be involved and sensitive, yet not lose yourself in your children. It isn't easy to be a parent and continue to be your own person.

As the parent of five children, I've known this for a long time. But I'd never talked about it until recently when a friend brought the subject up.

"I'm like tofu," she said wistfully. "I'm nourishing and all that—good for my children—but I pick up the flavor of whatever or whomever I'm around."

"But that's the advantage of tofu..." I argued.

"Yes, but I feel their feelings. When my kids are grouchy—I get grouchy. One was mildly depressed for awhile after an accident and I almost went under."

"You don't separate their feelings from your own," I echoed.

"Interests either..." she continued. "Whatever they're into at the moment—I pick up on."

"That sounds great to me."

"Not really—like I said—I'm tofu. Without any flavor of my own, I'm afraid I'm losing my identity—my personhood!"

I had to admit that was a problem.

How can you be a sensitive parent and still be **you**? Though difficult, it is quite possible. Here are some tips:

• Take care of yourself by meeting your own needs. Like the flight attendant says, "put on your own oxygen mask before putting on that of your children." What good to a child is a parent passed out from lack of oxygen? Though not so obviously drastic, the same principle applies to other basic needs. A needy person can't parent as well as one whose needs are met. Who, besides yourself, is going to take responsibility for your needs? Not your children. It's up to you!

• Be sensitive without getting sucked in. Sensitive people suffer the disappointment of others and feel their pain. They also

13

feel the elation and joy when it comes along. But you need to separate your feelings from those of your children. Stay aware of which are **your** pains, joys, sorrows, and which belong to your children. Don't numb yourself—stay sensitive—but sort out the feelings.

  • Keep your personal interests alive when you become a parent—you'll need them when your children grow up and are gone. Develop new ones as you go along, and not just ones that have to do with your children. Remain a well-rounded person.

Yes, tofu is enhanced by other flavors but it has its own unique flavor too, just like you. Learn to bring out your special flavor. Nurture your individuality. Stop blandly absorbing and start giving your flavor to the world around you.

7

GETTING IN TOUCH WITH WHO WE ARE

I had a dream.

I sat in an attic before a dusty trunk with its lid open. Inside I could see a small wooden box. I reached in and picked it up. The box felt empty. I took off the lid. Inside was a wash cloth carefully wrapped around an object. Curious as to what could have been put away like this, I took out the nearly weightless bundle and held it in my hand. I pulled back the cloth. I drew a gasp of shock. In my hand lay a tiny baby. I recognized this baby. Only at that moment did I remember that my son had been born with a twin but I had forgotten all about the second baby while I was lavishing my love, care, and affection on the first. Now here was the child, come to light, from the spot where I had hidden it long before.

As I looked on this practically mummified creature, its little chest began to heave as if I had breathed life into it by merely opening the box. My heart beat faster providing energy for this awakening child. My face flushed as its own little face turned from gray to white to pink. Before my eyes the tiny bundle I held in my hand came to life. I felt great joy!

I had this dream. Then I had it again. This must mean something, I told myself—the self who seldom dreams vivid dreams, let alone remembers them.

What could this dream mean? I could interpret it to mean that as a parent it's easy to neglect a child. Truly, that's a fear I hold deep down. But the joy I felt was the main quality of the dream—its message. Instead of the horror of neglect, I felt the joy of renewal.

My friend, a dream analyst, explained, "Maybe this dream isn't about a baby at all but about you. Perhaps there is a part of you that you have neglected. But obviously you have the power to breathe life into it again. Just see what power you have!"

It's true. I have more than one neglected part—so do all parents. There's no way to parent and still give expression to everything else in you. Some things have to be put on hold when you have the responsibility of raising children.

But what is this part of me that I've got on hold? What could I have so carefully wrapped up and tucked away and forgotten? I tried to find out.

Everyday I made it a point to focus just for a few minutes on this baby in the box from my dream. I'm not much of a meditator, so whenever I had a quiet moment I just thought about the baby—brought the image to my mind. I waited for the big revelation. But this is real life, and no revelation came—there was no dramatic "aha" that led me down new avenues of my being. Instead what came was the gradual knowledge and awareness of how many parts of me there are—some expressed and some not expressed.

And what I learned from the dream is that when it comes time to express a part I have stored away for the time being, it will come to life; its chest will heave, it will turn pink, and it will be viable. When the time is right, I have the power to bring life all the parts of me, even the hidden, neglected ones. So do you.

II

PARENTING SKILLS

When you really listen, you teach your
children an important communication skill.

Photo credit: Cris Evans

8

LEARNING NEW TECHNIQUES

Like playing the piano or shooting baskets, skill-building takes practice. Parenting skills are no exception.

While you're working to improve something, feedback is vital. Luckily, my children are always most eager to let me know how well I'm doing when I'm learning parenting techniques. I don't even have to ask. I know I've mastered a technique when my children don't notice it anymore.

Take the time I first started using "active listening." (Active listening is a means of reflecting back the emotion a child is displaying so the child feels "heard.")

My twelve year old son was blind with fury over some small incident and I remarked, "I can relate to your irritation."

"Don't use that psychology talk with me," he hissed through clenched teeth. "You sound like such a phony! Besides, I'm not irritated, I'm *mad*!"

I blew it that time but I didn't give up. Instead, I practiced and got better until I was so smooth that my children didn't recognize when I was using active listening and when I was just being my old natural self.

Even when I'm good at a technique, it takes my children some getting used to. For example, I was working on "conflict-resolution", a method of helping children talk through and sort out a conflict. I had honed my skills at preschool but hadn't tried them at home until the day when two neighborhood four-year-olds were arguing over a Tonka truck in my back yard. My own four-year-old was standing on the sidelines watching them—and me.

I walked over to the two boys tugging on the truck and using a calm, matter-of-fact voice, I said, "I see you both want the same truck." The boys turned to look at me.

"I had it first," screamed one.

"Talk to him about it," I said, indicating the other child.

They continued to make me the focus point. "It's my truck..." sobbed the other child looking directly at me.

"I see how unhappy you are. Tell him, not me." Again I put the argument back into the hands of the two children.

I was surprised at how fast the two took up my cues, argued it out, and went back to playing contently. My carefully practiced conflict resolution skills had worked!

I was basking in the glory of my success when I realized my son was looking at me with his mouth wide open. "Mommy, how come you were talking so funny?" he asked.

I did sound funny to him—not because I wasn't good at what I was doing but because it was new to him. He was more used to my old way of handling conflicts.

Of course, when I'm pushed to the end of my rope, I still stomp around, whine, and fuss like I used to. I know that I have other choices, though—not ones that come naturally but ones I've learned.

Parenting is a skill—one we learn as we go along—from books, from classes, from other parents. Skills take practice. None of us ever starts out perfect. We don't end up perfect either but we get better if we work at it.

9

LISTENING: A COMMUNICATION SKILL

Eight-year-old Jessica comes into the family room, throws her backpack on the couch, and then flops down beside it moaning: "I hate that old teacher! She gave me a test that was impossible and when I couldn't do it, I just wanted to die!"

Her mother, glaring at the backpack on the couch, responds. "Oh, come on now, don't be so dramatic. If you failed at a test, it's your own fault for not studying hard enough. And don't you ever say you hate someone. That's not nice! Now get up and go put that backpack where it belongs!"

Jessica slouches off pouting, leaving her backpack on the couch.

I wonder why it's so hard for parents to listen to their children and acknowledge their feelings. I know it is hard for me. Like Jessica's mother I tend to cut off the conversation with criticism, orders, admonitions, and advice. I put my focus on formulating my own answers instead of really listening to my children's words or what is behind them.

Sometimes I don't even listen long enough to know what the problem is; I jump to conclusions. I'm not alone in this approach to coping with my children's feelings. I regularly observe other parents taking the same approach.

Perhaps our children's feelings are too painful for us, so we discount them. Perhaps we feel we must teach every minute, making a lesson out of each situation. Maybe, without thinking about it, we just respond to our children the way our parents responded to us.

Imagine the Jessica conversation as it might have been if her mother had really been listening.

"I hate that old teacher," says Jessica throwing the backpack.

"Which teacher?" asks her mother ignoring both the word "hate" and the backpack.

"My P. E. teacher..." answers Jessica.

"You're really mad at her..." Her mother puts the feelings into words.

"Yes, she gave us this physical fitness test today and it was too hard." Jessica looks as though she's about to cry.

"You feel bad because you didn't do well on the test."

"I sure do. I was the first one, and everyone was watching me but I just couldn't do it! Some of the kids laughed at me."

"It's awful to be laughed at," her mother commiserates with her.

"I think they were just nervous because they were going to have to do it too. But they didn't have to because the teacher discovered she was giving me the sixth grade test. No wonder I couldn't pass it—I'm not a sixth grader!" A tear rolls down her cheek.

"Your teacher made a mistake and gave you the wrong test..." Her mother rewards the information.

"Yes, it was a pretty bad mistake." Jessica takes the tissue her mother offers. "I tried and tried but I just couldn't do it! I felt awful." Jessica looks as though she is starting to feel better now.

"I can imagine how you felt." Her mother sounds sincere.

Getting up abruptly from the couch, Jessica ends the conversation with a big sniff and the words, "Well, I gotta call Julie. I told her I'd call when I got home." Picking up her backpack, Jessica runs off satisfied that she has been heard.

How different this conversation was from the original version! What a relief to be heard instead of criticized and ordered about.

And the best part of all, really listening is an investment. When you really listen, you teach your children an important communication skill and one of these days, maybe you'll find the tables turned and they'll be **really listening to you!**

10

TEACH CHILDREN TO SOLVE THEIR OWN PROBLEMS

If children are to experience their own
sense of power, they need opportunities
to learn and practice all sorts of skills.

Photo credit: Jim Darter

20

Sometimes I look like a bad parent. Instead of being dependable, available, and kind, I seem to be uncaring and disinterested. I even believe in neglecting children.

"Oh, oh," you say. "Call the police!"

Wait a minute, hear me out. I don't mean neglecting children's needs—as a parent you have a legal, moral, and biological obligation to meet the needs of your children—physical, emotional, social, and intellectual needs. When they are babies, that's your job, or when you aren't around to do it, it's your job to find a substitute need-meeter. But as children grow older it's also your obligation to teach them to meet their own needs so that eventually they can take over your job entirely. Here's where the neglect comes in. Actually it starts in infancy as you teach babies to tune in to and express what they need.

Instead of jumping up at the first little simmering whimper my babies made, I let them come to a full rolling boil. If baby's every squeak is immediately answered with a nipple full of warm milk, they have no chance to really experience needs, let alone find ways to cope with a few minutes delay in getting them met. Of course, I don't mean that I used to let my babies scream their lungs out for long periods when hungry or any other time. That doesn't just look neglectful—it is neglectful. I mean I delayed my response just a bit sometimes.

The issue is one of empowerment. If children are to experience their own sense of power, they need opportunities to learn and practice all sorts of skills. They do that when parents step back a little sometimes. That includes letting a baby express his hunger clearly and cope with a small amount of deprivation. It also includes letting children do something you could easily do for them, like pouring milk or getting something from the refrigerator.

I remember a time in a park when I was watching my three-year-old try to climb a ledge in order to get up to something he couldn't reach. He was struggling but I stood back and kept my hands off him. A woman watching from nearby rushed over and lifted him up, saying as she did so, "There, now you can reach." Then she gave me a dirty look and left. I'm sure she classified me as a lazy or just plain **mean** mother. She misunderstood my motives.

Of course I'm not advocating that parents ignore their children. Children need attention. At the same time, they must learn to express, cope with, and meet their own needs.

When the end is in sight of your child-rearing responsibilities—when your children are at a leaving-home age—it becomes even more important to be a "bad" parent. Don't be always available, dependable, and kind. It's too hard to grow up and leave a good parent. Imagine yourself in the position of having your mom or your dad as your best support system, your listening ear, your dearest friend. How could you ever leave such a person? Some young people, in fact, when faced with this dilemma become so difficult to live with that they force their parents to quit being so wonderful.

So now you know that I'm proud to look like a bad parent. I'm purposely stepping back, leaving my hands off, in order for my children to grow into skillful, independent people able to meet their own needs.

USING THE TEACHABLE MOMENT

A teachable moment.

Photo credit: Jim Darter

A parent with preschool-age twins caught my eye in the grocery store. She and her children were having a great time together. This mother obviously had scheduled a chunk of time for shopping and was leisurely strolling the aisles. She stopped her cart when her children showed an interest in something. She answered their questions. She paid attention to them.

I decided this family was worth observing, so I surreptitiously hung out by the lettuce, watching as she let them help her pick a cantaloupe by pressing and smelling the stem end. They discussed which cantaloupe felt the softest and smelled the ripest.

I puttered around a pyramid of cans while farther down the aisle she talked about which kind of juice each boy preferred and showed them how to "read" the pictures on the outside of the can to know what's inside.

This mother showed a wonderful understanding of how to use what's called the teachable moment. She was tuned in to her children. She was responsive to their questions and comments, as well as pointing out things for them to think about.

The most effective education for young children, perhaps for all of us, is taking advantage of those moments when the "student" is alert, calm, interested, and motivated. You can put a good deal of effort into trying to get your children into that state, or you can spend your time paying attention so you know when they are already there and open to learning.

Just being able to recognize a teachable moment isn't enough. You have to be flexible about how children's interest changes, what they are capable of understanding, and most of all—how to let go of the lesson when they've had enough.

I remember listening to a mother and her toddler in a laundromat. (Watch out for me, I'm always lurking about observing people.) This little guy asked a simple question about the change-making machine. The mother saw a teachable moment and went for it. But instead of just answering his questions, she started a lengthy lecture on math, economics, and how things work. She asked a million questions and answered them all herself. "See, four quarters come out; four quarters make a dollar. How many nickels make a quarter? Five." The child fiddled with a shoelace. Ten minutes later, she was still at it. "Here's where we put the quarters. Do you know why we need quarters?" Yak, yak, yak. The child played with a pile of spilled soap on the floor the whole time she gave her speech.

This mother was trying too hard and she missed the mark.

Let's look at another example of a teachable moment gone astray. This example is a made-up one. Here's a toddler imitating her mother who is clearing off the table. The child takes a plate when her mother has her back turned. Unfortunately, she drops it and it breaks. Her angry mother turns around and gives her a whack, then sends her away. The teachable moment is lost. Instead of sorting out what went wrong, and learning to carry plates so they don't drop, her daughter focuses on the smack and her feelings about it. Because she's now in the other room, she doesn't learn how to respond if a plate does break and needs to be swept up. She did learn something but not what her mother would have wanted her to learn if she had thought about it. The lesson she learned was two-fold: One, helping can get you in trouble; two, it's not okay to make a mistake.

Right after a mishap is when children are most open to learning a lesson. Rather than helping them sort out what happened, parents can interfere with the lesson by doing something drastic in the name of discipline.

We parents are teachers every moment of our waking lives whether we're sweeping up broken plates or just walking through the grocery store with our children. It's important that we give some thought to what we teach and how we teach it.

IN THE FACE OF A POWER
STRUGGLE: DISENGAGE

Parents and children are like gears. They can either engage or disengage.

You don't have to stay in drive all the time. You can shift into neutral. A car in neutral is still running but doesn't move. You can idle or rev up but as long as the gears are not engaged, they don't affect each other and the car stays calmly in place.

This is a useful concept if you are inclined to get into power struggles with your child. As the adult, you are like the driver of the car who must be the one to decide when to engage and when to disengage the gears.

Engage when you have the power to steer your child toward cooperative instead of submissive behavior. Engagement should result in a win-win outcome. Figure out ways that both you and your child benefit from the outcome. Don't try to win at the expense of your child. When in that situation, *disengage*!

I watched my cousin with her eighteen-month-old son who was constantly doing things he shouldn't. What she was doing was much like a dance. She and her son moved together beautifully, until something would pop up to create friction. For example, he wanted to empty the wastebasket onto the floor. She knew how to remain engaged and use her power to skillfully redirect his energy to his bucket of blocks. "Not the wastebasket, empty this instead," she suggested without getting either pushy or mad.

I wasn't always that good when I had little kids. I'd often find myself in a confrontation where I felt I had to win. I'd have a lot at stake including my own sense of power. With my teeth gritted, I'd charge forward determined to impose my will. I'd feel a great need to control one of my children. It must have been a funny sight to see a grown woman taking on a tiny little kid but it didn't feel funny. We'd both be so determined to win that it would get ugly.

Parents can't win power struggles. Oh sure, you can overpower your child sometimes but even when you win, you lose. You lose because either the child gets back at you using the energy of his or her built-up resentment to win the next round, or he gives up and comes to see himself as a loser. If he wins the next round, he learns that it's fun to defeat you, which sets you both up for a further round of head-on engagements. Worse, if he never wins, you then defeat your own purpose by convincing him that he's a loser.

I don't want my children to feel overpowered, I want them to feel *empowered*, but that's hard to accomplish when I get myself into win/lose situations.

It takes a lot of awareness, will power, and skill to disengage in the face of a battle; but it's worth it.

If power struggles are your problem, ask yourself these questions next time you're in the middle of one:

- Is this really a significant matter? (Usually it isn't—it's the principle of the thing.) If you can't find another way to solve problems, at least save the power struggles for the really big issues. Don't engage over every little thing.

- Why is your need to overpower your child so great? Are you trying to make up for your own powerless childhood? Do you really want your child to be in the same position you were?

- Most of all ask yourself, what can I do to disengage when in a power struggle? How do I put this machine in neutral? You may have your own techniques. I've found that the element of surprise works. Do the unexpected to break the hold. Humor also helps me disengage. Mostly, it's the awareness that disengagement is possible. I remember this by holding an image of gears in my head.

13

STOP BUTTON-PUSHING BY BEING INCONSISTENT

Everyone tells you that parents have to be consistent. It's easy to agree when you think in terms of doing what you say you'll do. But I always resist hard fast rules. Maybe I just never did grow up but whenever someone presents me with a rule, I present that person with an argument. Let me tell you my story so you'll understand why I believe in both consistency **and inconsistency** as parenting approaches.

I look like a regular person but I'm not. I'm really a robot with about a million little buttons located just under my skin in various positions all over my body. My children, at birth, began memorizing the position of each and every one of these buttons. By two years of age, each knew exactly what it took to activate those buttons. If they had an IQ test to measure button-pushing abilities, my children would all fall in the genius range. I don't mean to brag but those little kids were **smart**.

Button-pushing works this way. The child performs some small behavior (which has been tried previously and proved to be effective). The parent responds in some completely predictable fashion, setting off a pattern that is extremely familiar to both child and parent—one they've both been through many times before.

Here is an example. My daughter, at 13, could activate my buttons with a single word. I would say something I felt was important and I wanted her to think was important too. She would respond with a bored look on her face. "So......?" she'd say in a most disrespectful way. I always took her response to mean—"That's the stupidest thing I ever heard—what do I care anyway..."

That little word "so" would always result in a fight. I'd start by saying, through gritted teeth, that she never listened to me and that she didn't care about anything. She'd respond defensively and we'd be off and running until eventually we were both yelling awful accusations at each other. I don't think I ever failed to react in my predictable way. She could count on me to set this pattern in motion! I was consistent!

The secret to bypassing the pattern is to be **inconsistent**—to respond in a surprising way. Looking back on it, I see how I could have altered my response. I could have ignored her answer and changed the subject. I could have just walked away. I could have written her a note saying how I felt. I could have tried an assertive response. If I were really good at surprises, I could have laughed. What I know now (yet continually forget) is that all it takes to break a pattern is to make some small change in your typical response. It's surprising how hard that is to do!

So I want to go on record as supporting consistency **when appropriate** but cheering on those who learn to become real people instead of robots—those who refuse to respond predictably when their buttons are pushed! I'm not all the way there yet; I'm still part robot but I at least see the possibility of becoming fully human.

14

LIFE IS ABOUT CHOICES

I believe in giving children choices. Lots of benefits occur when children have choices. Power struggles subside as they resist you less. With an increased sense of power, children spend less energy grabbing for it and more energy being cooperative. Children also learn about the consequences of their choices. This lesson is one of the most important ones any of us ever learn, and we get more and more skilled at choosing the consequences we need and want than those we don't.

What do I mean by giving choices? Say you're trying to get your toddler into the bathtub and you're getting resistance. Instead of saying "get into the tub *now*" and hearing him shout "*no!*", try giving a choice. Ask, "Do you want to take your bath before dinner or after dinner?" Suppose he makes his choice for after dinner, and the time comes for the bath and he's still resisting, what do you do then? Give a choice. Say, "Do you want to climb into the tub yourself or shall I put you in?" In this way you remain in charge but the child still has a sense of power because he can control the situation to some extent.

It's amazing how well this approach works. Most of the time, children don't think of rejecting both choices but pick one or the other. Even for something as distasteful as taking medicine, a choice works. Ask, "Do you want to drink it out of the yellow glass or the blue glass?" or "Do you want to hold the spoon yourself or shall I hold it for you?"

Sometimes the choice is between doing something or suffering the consequences of not doing it. Feeding the pet guinea pig may be something you and your child fight over. You don't have to get into a power struggle. The choice is rather simple. Animals who aren't fed, die. Neglecting animals is immoral (as well as illegal), therefore, people who neglect animals have them taken away. You don't need to call in the SPCA, just give the guinea pig away. There's bound to be a child care program nearby who would love to have your guinea pig.

Of course, the urge is to rescue—rescue the guinea pig; rescue the child. That's okay if you're willing to take on the responsibility for this pet. But be clear that is what you are doing. And when your child begs for a puppy the next week, don't expect her to feed it for more than a couple of days. Realize what you have taught her: The consequence of not feeding a pet is that mom or dad takes over. No matter what you say, this lesson is now ingrained in your child.

Yes, life is about choices and children need to learn that at a young age. You'll know you've been successful when they not only learn to make choices but also to give them. For example, I was surprised one afternoon when I picked up my son, Timmy, from nursery school. He climbed into his car seat and waited for me to buckle him in. Then, looking me straight in the eye, he announced in a clear, firm voice, "You have two choices, Mom. You can either take me home or take me to the store and buy me a toy."

III

DISCIPLINE

Effective discipline depends on a good relationship.

Photo credit: Jim Darter

PARENTS AS ALLIES

When you're disciplining your child, do you see yourself on her side or do you see the two of you on opposite sides? This is an important question. The more you butt heads during the times you are guiding your child's behavior, the harder it will be to make positive changes.

It's a matter of attitude. Take, for example, this instance. Your four-year-old is out of control. She is pounding on her little sister when you arrive on the scene. You're furious! You grab her roughly by the arm. She resists you; flailing and kicking. You feel like hitting her to teach her a lesson. You decide not to because you know that you would be modeling the very behavior you're trying to extinguish. Instead, you drag her to the time-out chair where you give her an indeterminate sentence. She struggles to get up. You hold her down. You scold her but she ignores you. You make her sit there extra long because you are so mad and because she shows no signs of repenting. You finally give up, let her up with a stern warning, and keep your fingers crossed that the problem is solved. (Maybe it is—maybe it isn't. If you're wise you'll hang around a bit longer to see what happens next.)

Now I'm not condemning you for taking this approach or for feeling what you were feeling—I'm certainly no angel myself. What I just described was a very human, even sort of humane, approach to stopping unacceptable behavior. But it's not the most effective approach because you and your child became adversaries instead of partners.

Here's a better approach (**when** you can manage it).

You arrive on the scene to see the pounding going on. Anger rises. (That's usually my first response to this kind of situation.) You step aside from the anger. You may or may not choose to express it first with something like, "I feel really upset when I see you hurting your sister." Expressed or not, it's important to put your anger aside in order to deal with the situation in a helpful, rather than hurtful, way.

You take hold of your child who continues flailing and kicking—totally lacking in control. You want to talk to her about her sister's feelings but right now she can't relate to anyone else's feelings—she's too wrapped up in her own. You say to her in a firm but unemotional voice, "I see you need my help right now to control your behavior." You remove her from the scene and find a place where she can concentrate on getting back into control. (This can be her room since you are helping her, not punishing her.) If she can calm herself without you, fine. If she needs you there, stay. You may be needed to provide her with a clear, calm focus. Just sitting quietly and concentrating on your own breathing may help her tune into your rhythms and bring her out of her frenzy. You may be able to help her to a calm state without touching her. If you can't, you may need to hold her firmly. Face her outward—away from you—so that she isn't distracted by trying to relate to you. Don't scold or try to teach her any lessons at this time. What she needs right now is a quiet presence to help her focus.

This works! Once she has gotten hold of herself, you can bring her back out to the other room to deal with what happened and talk about feelings. At this point, you can work at problem-solving, as well as give some guidelines about future behavior.

Best of all...instead of being angry with you, she'll be appreciative that you helped her at a time she most needed it. Being out of control is as frightening for the child experiencing it as it is for the target of the out-of-control behavior. Children need help at these times—not punishment.

_____ **16** _____

CONSEQUENCES NOT PUNISHMENT

It's possible, and indeed desirable, to raise children without punishing them. Children learn to behave in many ways. One is by following your lead and imitating your behavior. (Punishment works against you there.) Another is by discovering the consequences of their own actions.

Here's an example of how children learn through experiencing consequences. One of my children was lazy about putting his dishes in the dishwasher—lazy to the point of stubbornness. I'd remind him, nag him—I even resorted to threatening but nothing worked. Finally, when I gave up, I'd always put his dirty dishes away.

Then I decided to use the natural consequence approach. I asked myself, what is the ultimate consequence of not putting dirty dishes in the dishwasher? I visualized a house full of molding dishes. Would my child mind that? Then I visualized an empty cupboard—no dishes for the next meal: the ultimate consequence. Even if the dirty house didn't affect him, the empty cupboard would.

So I explained to my son that I wouldn't remind or nag anymore but I wouldn't put his dishes away either. And I didn't. Neither did he! By bedtime the first day, the place was a dump but my son didn't seem to mind. I got impatient. How long was this going to take anyway?

I decided to hurry the process along by adding to the problem. I quit putting my dishes away, too.

The next morning I left my coffee cup on the newspaper by my rocking chair, my cereal bowl and juice glass on the table, and an empty water glass on the wood stove next to the two empty glasses my son had left there the previous day.

It didn't take long. We never got to the point of the bare cupboard. He didn't like the mess once it got really ugly. He picked up his dishes, I picked up mine, and that was the end of it.

How does this approach differ from punishment? For one thing, I didn't inflict anything on him. I merely quit doing what hadn't worked before and let his own actions show him the problem. He learned a lesson about the benefits of household order without being punished. I was a bystander—not a moralizer, judge, or jury. I even managed to refrain from saying, "I hope you learned your lesson."

Punishment has many disadvantages. If you do something that hurts, the child becomes more wrapped up in his own pain and in his feelings about you than in the lesson to be learned.

Young children who are punished for mistakes and wrong-doings (many of which are mistakes) tend to explore and experiment less. Again, learning is reduced. Many children come to see new situations as dangerous rather than as opportunities to use their initiative to find out more about the world around them.

Punishment may cause fear or resentment, and those feelings tear down relationships between parents and children. **Effective discipline depends on good relationships.** Once resentment starts, it creates a vicious cycle. Just like modern germs build resistance to medicine, so does the resentful child become resistant to punishment. That means parents must make the next dose stronger. Some children are willing to take a lot, so the parent continues to escalate in retaliation. It's easy to end up abusing a child when caught up in this ugly pattern.

All this infliction of pain and deprivation is very different from kindly and firmly allowing children to experience the consequences of their own actions. Discipline by using consequences isn't easy. It takes skill and sensitivity to keep consequences from turning into punishments. Work on developing those skills and preserve the relationship with your child. It's worth the effort!

————— **17** —————

STOP RESCUING!

Feedback is a great teaching device. It differs from praise and criticism in that it is nonjudgmental. Feedback is what computers give—word processors as well as video games. Something either works or it doesn't. No one yells at you or purposely makes you feel bad. That may be the appeal that computers and computer games have for children. (Adults, too!)

You certainly don't have to have a computer to use feedback for a teaching tool. I only used that as an example because the computer's **immediate nonjudgmental feedback** is excellent for learning. Computers aside, feedback is constant in everything we do. Sometimes we seek it. We test things out—like tasting the hot chocolate to see if 1½ minutes in the microwave is long enough. Other times feedback comes upon us unexpectedly. We put an oversized wool sweater in the drier and remove a mini-sweater an hour later. Feedback that teaches occurs naturally in situations every day.

Here are some examples of children learning through feedback. Busy Jamie skips watering the bean seed she planted in preschool. The sprout withers. Amy forgets to set her alarm clock. By the time she wakes up, she's missed walking with her best friend and has to run with the last-minute neighbor child. Jason shoves his dirty jeans under the bed every evening instead of putting them in the clothes hamper. When the last pair is gone from his drawer, he is left with getting some outgrown jeans out of the Goodwill bag. Brian notices the tank is on empty when he borrows his dad's car to go to a football game. He ignores that fact until he runs out of gas. He misses the first touchdown because of the time it took to walk to the gas station and back to the car.

A common pattern is for parents to rush in and save the children from their own actions or inactions and then feel angry that their children don't do what they should. Mom nags Jamie about watering, then finally does it herself. Dad constantly reminds Amy about setting her alarm, then when she forgets he wakes her up. Dad yells about the dirty clothes under Jason's bed, then gets up early to wash the morning Jason runs out of jeans. Mom brings her car to Brian so he can get to the game on time, then calls her friend to bring her some gas.

I'm not saying parents should never perform these kind acts for their children. But rescuing often becomes a pattern, one that makes children dependent and parents angry. Once parents perceive they are in this pattern, it's time to look at the lesson they are teaching. When rescue occurs, the only feedback the child gets is that Mom or Dad will take care of everything. The potential for learning responsibility goes right down the drain along with the feedback.

Children learn from their own actions. They don't need nagging or blaming for the lesson to come through. They may feel temporarily disappointed, hurt, and angry; but they learn. And after all, **learning** is the goal of discipline.

WHAT'S YOUR GOAL—
OBEDIENCE OR COOPERATION?

If you use a problem-solving approach,
you'll find children feel more powerful
and are more willing to cooperate.

Photo credit: Jim Darter

"My kids never listen to me," is a complaint I often hear from parents. I'm beginning to wonder if evolution has left the next generation with a hearing problem. Perhaps our ears are becoming useless appendages only good for displaying earrings!

Wrong! The problem isn't in our children's ears; it's in their motivation system. And the problem isn't theirs—it's ours.

What do parents really mean when they say, "My kids never listen to me"? They mean, "When I tell my children to do something, they don't do it." If you ask them to elaborate, they'll give an example such as, "I tell my son to take out the trash and he just keeps on reading like he didn't hear a word I said."

If your kids don't listen to you, here's what I suggest. Explore the problem a bit more. Start by thinking about what exactly it is that you want from your children. Is it really obedience you're after? Sure, it would be easier if we could issue an order and our kids would respond like little soldiers. But do you really want your kids to obey someone's orders all their lives? I don't. I want them to think for themselves. After all, I can't be sure those giving the orders—those in authority over my children—will always be benevolent.

My goal is not obedience and compliance but cooperation. I want my children to learn that they are better off when they are cooperative than when they are not. How do I teach this lesson?

First of all, I have to become sensitive to my needs and those of my children whenever a problem arises and they "won't listen to me." I can express my needs and even my frustration. That gets things out in the open and may relieve me. But I can't expect **my** needs or even my anger to motivate my child. My children are wrapped up in their own needs.

My anger doesn't cause action on their part because that only works if they are **afraid** to displease me. Ruling by fear is not my goal. I certainly don't want my children to use their anger to control others, so I don't want to model that approach myself.

So how do I teach cooperation? How do I get my child to take out the trash, for example? I start by having a discussion about joint responsibility for shared living space. The discussion needs to be tuned to the age of the child in question. I'll also make sure I'm not mad when I start this discussion—because anger gives it a whole different complexion.

I will use a problem-solving approach, not a lecture, in this discussion. Together, we'll explore feelings and choices. We'll come to agreements on sharing responsibilities. We'll explore trade-offs. We'll decide on consequences when someone fails to do what he or she has agreed to.

I'm not saying your child will jump up from a good book and empty the trash if you follow my advice. I **am** saying that children feel more powerful, therefore more willing to cooperate, when they are part of a decision-making process. I'm willing to bet you'll find that, in general, their ears work better too!

_____ 19 _____

DON'T DEPEND ON WORDS ALONE

Tired of talking? Sometimes parents use too many words in the face of misbehavior. Parents talk, talk, talk and the kid keeps on doing whatever it is he's doing.

Words by themselves often won't change anything. What's needed is action.

Say your toddler is shoving a chair over to climb on the counter and you're trying to teach him to stay on the floor. If he doesn't respond to words alone, try action. Don't swat him—stop him. If he continues to try to shove the chair back, take it into the other room. If he persists with another chair—take **him** into the other room. You're bigger than he is. You can get your message across without hurting him. Talk to him while you are doing all this.

The baby plays in the toilet every time your back is turned. Two solutions come immediately to mind—a lock on the outside of the bathroom door. Or buy one of those gadgets that holds the cover of the toilet down. You won't have to deal with the behavior once you make the toilet water inaccessible.

Sometimes it's a simple matter of redirecting the child's energy. Your child wants to jump on the couch—you send her out to jump on the old inner tube in the back yard, physically guiding her if words don't work. Or she's mad at her brother and ready to hit him. You take her to a punching bag in the garage. (A garbage bag full of rags works just as well and can be kicked, stomped, and jumped upon as well as hit.)

Talking by itself may not be an effective response to misbehavior. Parental action is often called for but sometimes parental **inaction** is the solution. Consider the following situation.

Your kindergartner is slow getting ready for school every day. You constantly push, urge, threaten, and finally end up doing things for her that she should be doing for herself. You're determined that she should never be late to school and you make it your responsibility to see that she isn't.

One day, however, you decide to let her experience the consequences of being late. You tell her that it's up to her to be ready on time. She plays her same old tricks, only this time you don't fall for them. You do nothing to help her get ready. You simply wait. She takes her time. **Finally**, she's ready for school and you take her. She walks in forty-five minutes late and causes a bit of a stir with the interruption, which embarrasses her. She discovers she missed milk money collection—so won't get milk at snack time. She also missed show-and-tell and it was her day! The puppet who discusses the weather has finished. She loves that puppet! She feels unhappy.

The next morning things are different. You don't need lots of words **or** actions to get her ready on time. Your inaction yesterday did the trick. She experienced the consequences of being late. Today she's motivated!

A final word of advice. Just because words alone don't always work, don't leave out the words when you use either an action or inaction approach. You should always communicate what you are doing and why. You don't have to go on and on but it is worthwhile to provide reasons. That way children can eventually do their own reasoning as they look at their behavior and make choices about it.

By talking to your children, while guiding their behavior, you enhance the relationship. A good relationship helps any discipline approach be more effective and results in more positive outcomes.

USE TALK INSTEAD OF SWAT

I read an article about how the police use negotiators in critical situations before the S.W.A.T. team strikes. The point of the article was that in life-threatening situations, a talker goes in to see if the problem can be solved through negotiation, rather than getting out the big guns and blowing the person off the face of the earth.

"Aha!" I said to myself. That approach applies to parenting as well! If we all used **talk** instead of "S.W.A.T." with our children, the world would be a different place!

Parents, of course, don't face situations where they must blow their children off the face of the earth in order to save the population at large. However, they often use painful adult force—big guns—that would be unnecessary if they believed in talk. Once they understand the power of negotiation, of a "problem-solving approach," they can ban the big guns forever.

I am not suggesting that parents don't need back-up. They do. But they have it automatically. Their back-up is the power that comes from their superior intelligence and greater experience, as well as their size and strength. They can choose to use that power **for** the child, rather than **on** the child. Back-up, used properly, helps rather than hurts the child.

How can you use "talk"? Think in terms of R-E-R-U-N: **R**eflect, **E**xplain, **R**eason, **U**nderstand, **N**egotiate—all words that involve talking.

• **Reflect.** Let your child know that his or her feelings are received and accepted by you. Reflect them with words such as, "I see how unhappy you are" or "I can tell you are very angry."

• **Explain.** Help the child understand the situation. "I can't let you run in the street."

• **Reason.** Give the reason for your prohibition. "You might get hurt."

• **Understand.** Tune in to feelings—both yours and the child's. Really understand the situation from both points of view.

You don't have to say anything at this point, just be sure you have clarity. You may have to talk to yourself to get it.

- **Negotiate.** Now is the time for problem-solving. If the child is old enough to talk, you can discuss the problem and together find a mutually satisfying solution. If the child is too young for talking it out, try giving the child some alternatives. "You can stay up here on the porch, or you can play in the back yard."

I don't mean you should talk every situation to death. Notice the few words used in the r-e-r-u-n sequence above. The negotiations are the only part that need more than a brief phrase. With an older child, the negotiations can get lengthy but don't let it become a game. Keep your understanding of the true situation. When negotiations are breaking down, return to the beginning and go through the first four (R-E-R-U) parts again. You may have to R-E-R-U-N several times before the problem is solved. Be patient.

This all sounds fairly simple but it isn't easy. We're too used to reaching into the old hip holster when the going gets tough. You need both practice and patience to replace S.W.A.T. with R-E-R-U-N but the outcome is worth the effort it takes.

====== **21** ======

WAITING IS A LEGITIMATE PARENT MODE

Two important themes, two modes of being, run as threads through our parenting careers. I call these two modes **acting** and **waiting**.

Waiting is a theme of fairy tales. One story comes immediately to mind—*Sleeping Beauty*. This fairy tale contains a lesson for us, both men and women—and the lesson is not about Prince Charming. It's about waiting as a legitimate mode of being. It's about patience. It's about the heroism of **not** acting in some situations—but waiting it out instead.

Before I became a parent, I was an action person. In fact, the year before my first pregnancy was the fullest one of my life. I was finishing college in grand style—not only taking a heavy course load

42

but serving as president of several organizations. In addition, I took up skiing that year. Waiting was definitely not a theme of my life—then.

Imagine how my life changed when I got married, became pregnant, and moved to a foreign country. I was president of nothing, had no studying to do, couldn't work, and couldn't ski. I'll tell you—I was frustrated! Nine months of trying to entertain myself was a lifetime. I wasn't used to waiting. I was used to making things happen, to taking charge, to being in control. I was ripe for the first lesson of parenthood, which is, **some things you just can't make happen**. You can't control everything. You can't make a baby. You have to wait for it to grow.

When the grand climax arrived and the baby came into the world, I thought the waiting was over. Wrong. Then came the crying. Of course, I took action. I didn't just wait around for the crying to go away. Sometimes I could figure out what to do—the baby had some need to be met. But often the crying continued despite my actions. I was frustrated but I learned again about patience and waiting.

Night wakings were another arena where waiting was sometimes more useful than action. I learned to hold back when the first peep came because sometimes the baby put himself back to sleep. I didn't let him lie there screaming forever but I did learn to distinguish when waiting was the right approach and when a response from me was what he needed.

The two-year-old stage brought more lessons in patience and waiting. I waited out a lot of tantrums in my time—power struggles too. While a child is screaming "no" at you, it's best to let go rather than try to take charge. The more you try to control rebellion, the longer it lasts. I know—I tried heavy-duty action more than once. We always ended up in a struggle that made us both look like two-year-olds.

Just as you can't make a baby, you can't develop a child. Children unfold in their own time. It was frustrating to watch my neighbor's child unfold faster in her school-readiness skills than my own. This little girl spent hours with books and taught herself to read before kindergarten, while my own four-year-old spent his days riding his tricycle and digging in the sand. I backed off in a hurry when I discovered that pushing him toward early reading made us both nervous. I quit trying to develop him. I went back to the waiting mode.

Waiting is a major theme for parents of teenagers, as they wait for their children to get off the phone, come home at night, and outgrow the weird clothing, unusual hair styles, odd customs, and curious ways of talking.

Waiting is underrated as a parenting skill. The words that we use to describe someone in the waiting mode—words such as passive or inactive—are more negative than positive. These words indicate a lack rather than a value. But my message is that waiting is a legitimate mode of being. That's the way I look at Sleeping Beauty; she was doing just what she should have been doing. However, Sleeping Beauty was different from us parents. She lacked a choice. Waiting, appropriate as it is at times, is not all there is to life. Sometimes action is called for. The trick to good parenting is to know which mode is called for and how long to use it. Because we're awake, we can decide.

IV

PROBLEMS

Prevention is a key word in dealing with problems.

22

BITING

Screams filled the hallway of the child care program I was visiting. "Sounds like the gators are snapping again," remarked the director, who was showing me around. "That's the toddler room," she explained in answer to my questioning look. "I just hope Jaws isn't after Princess again," she added cryptically.

She went on to explain the alligator reference, "We call the toddlers 'the gators' because they are always biting each other." She ignored the "Jaws" and "Princess" reference, leaving me to figure it out.

She didn't have to tell me that toddlers bite. As a parent and an early childhood educator, I am well aware of that fact. I experienced the toddler stage five times at home and countless more times in the child care centers I've been associated with in my career.

Toddlers bite because they can't talk very well. They use their mouths in more direct ways to gain power.

Biting is a behavior that's easier to understand than to control. Yet control it you must—not after the fact but before it happens. **Prevention** is the key word. You wouldn't ignore a toddler with a loaded gun in his hand. Well, a mouth full of teeth, in some toddlers, is a lot like a loaded gun. Since you can't take the teeth away from him, you *have* to keep him from using them on people.

Here are four tips about how to prevent biting:

• Be vigilant. Whenever two toddlers are together and one of them has been known to bite, don't just let them play. Supervise closely. That isn't fun if you're there for some reason other than watching toddlers play but it's necessary. This need to supervise won't last forever—eventually the child who bites will learn other ways to express desires, get needs met, ask for attention, and feel powerful. But while learning these other ways, the child needs close supervision.

• Help toddlers feel powerful by giving choices; by offering challenges that take strength and skill. Feed those power feelings rather than denying them. When children are made to see themselves as small, weak, and inadequate, their power needs grow, sometimes to a monstrous size. The more helpless they feel, the more likely they are to use the strongest muscles in their little bodies—those that control the jaw!

• Provide the means to act out aggressions symbolically. Toy alligators can be useful for this purpose. Or try hand puppets that can "bite" without hurting.

• Teach toddlers how to defend themselves—to keep themselves from being bit. I don't mean by biting first or by slugging it out. The best way to explain is to write my own version of the story of "Jaws and the Princess" alluded to that day in the toddler program I visited.

Picture this: Princess is innocently playing with a yellow ball when along comes Jaws, a child who has bitten her many times in the past. Jaws wants the yellow ball—or perhaps he just wants another taste of Princess's tender arm. He approaches her, mouth open wide. But today is different. Princess is now armed with some non-violent self-defense skills.

First, she puts up one hand and says in her firmest toddler voice, "Stop!" At the same time, with the other hand, she takes a plastic teething ring out of her pocket. Stretching out her arm, she gently places the teething ring into the oncoming mouth. Surprised, Jaws bites down on it instead of her arm. That's the end of the story!

_____ **23** _____

LYING

Children sometimes say things that aren't true. We all do. We tell a joke. We make up a story for entertainment. We give an excuse. When we say things that aren't true for negative reasons, like avoiding blame, it's called a lie.

How can you keep children from lying? Here are some ideas about ways to look at lying and what to do about it.

Children are learning about the power of words and their ability to manipulate reality. They sometimes engage in wishful thinking, which means that they believe saying something is true **makes** it true. When they tell a lie, they may be more interested in changing reality than they are in trying to deceive you. If you understand this characteristic of young minds you'll deal with the situation less harshly than if you don't.

Young children are still learning to distinguish what's real from what's not. We hamper this learning when we don't separate fantasy from reality. So if we tell them that the tooth fairy put money under the pillow and pass that off as true, we can expect them to pass their fantasies off as true also. Fantasy isn't bad for children. However, when children are trying to sort things out, they may become frustrated with an adult who continues in fantasy under questioning. In addition, children may well imitate that same approach as an explanation of how things happen.

Sometimes a lie is really a difference in perception. When two children are arguing, each may firmly believe his or her own version of the story. It doesn't help for an adult to step in and decide which is the truth and which is a lie. It is more useful for the adult to help the children sort it out themselves. The adult can encourage them to give each other feedback and invite them to explain their own perceptions to each other. This kind of situation provides excellent practice for problem-solving and conflict-resolution skills. Let children learn these skills young. Don't decide for them what happened and who was right and who was wrong. You won't have to deal with lies if you let them sort out their disagreements themselves without taking sides.

Here are three tips for dealing with a child who is telling something different from the truth you believe:

- Understand young children's fuzzy line between fantasy and reality. They don't perceive the world in the same way an adult does. Gently help them sort out the truth.

- Be truthful yourself. Honesty is taught best through modeling. If you say there's no more dessert when the refrigerator's full of it, you're teaching lying. If you model that kind of behavior, you must expect children to engage in it as well.

- Don't back children into a corner when you know they've done wrong or made a mistake. Don't ask, "Who did this?" if you already know. Most children will try to save face or escape a consequence by going off into fantasyland. The younger ones may not even know that's what they are doing.

In conclusion, a sensitive, understanding approach is more effective than heavy-handed confrontation when dealing with children who depart from the truth. And who knows—maybe their reality is more valid than ours anyway!

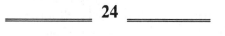

24

BATHROOM TALK

Why are small children so obsessed with bathroom language? It gets really old hearing them talk about body parts and body functions all day if you don't understand why they do it.

Children talk about what interests them. Body functions preoccupy young children because they are learning to control them.

But it's more than just intense interest. Young children explore words just as they explore objects. When they learn the words that relate to the parts of their bodies that use the toilet (and the products that come out of these body parts) they are intrigued. They try the words out, they play with them. They even invent new ones.

Children start out by using bathroom words without knowing what is appropriate and what is not. They hear the words and they imitate what they hear. They acquire these words the way they acquire the rest of their vocabulary.

If, while they are playing, they discover that these sounds (and after all—that's all they are) cause a great disturbance, they are going to use them over and over again.

Yelling "butt face" at a playmate may create a huge furor as the child reacts to the insult. Whispering "shit" behind a parent's back causes her to whirl around suddenly and focus a good deal of attention on the culprit.

These experiences teach young children what we adults already know. Words have power—they can excite. They can also calm, soothe, and heal—but more importantly to the young child, they can insult, hurt, annoy, irritate, and infuriate.

It makes sense that when little children discover the power of words, they want to use the most powerful ones they can find.

So what can you do about "cleaning up" a child's mouth? Forget the old-fashioned soap mouthwash. There are far better ways that don't harm or degrade the child. Here are some suggestions:

• The first time your child says something you disapprove of, make a brief statement about its inappropriateness. This statement alone may do it. But if the word has already gained power, then you have to take its power away by ignoring it.

• If the behavior is primarily designed to get your attention, ignoring it will make it go away. There's no reward in yelling "poopoo head" at someone who turns and walks away. Your response takes away the power of that particular word. Of course, once won't do it—the child is bound to test again and again—especially if he or she has gotten a response in the past. Eventually, you can suck the word of its energy by taking your attention away from it.

• Give the child some substitute words to use, ones that you can tolerate. One mother taught her son the Latin derivative words "defecate," "urinate," "feces," and so forth. He did avoid the Anglo-Saxon four letter words as well as the baby talk words his friends were using but he took as much relish in playing with his bathroom words as the next kid. He got attention for the little insults and chants he made up—but seemed to offend fewer people either because they didn't understand or because he was so cute. He eventually outgrew the need to use these words for entertainment.

• If you can set some limits without initiating a big power struggle, you can also try that approach. This should be done without a big fuss or you further reinforce the behavior. Some families assign a special place where any kind of talk is allowed. "Go to the bathroom for bathroom talk" is a rule in some homes.

Whatever you do, stay out of power struggles. As in toilet training, you're in for big trouble if you take a heavy-handed approach to trying to control what comes out of your children. You'll be sorry. Instead, focus on finding ways to grant them their power while keeping yours!

25

TESTING LIMITS

The only way children know where
parental limits lie is by testing them.

Photo credit: Jim Darter

Child development experts use jargon words such as "limits" and "testing." Parents seldom use these words—instead they talk about rules and discipline and misbehavior. Although the concepts are similar, the images are slightly different.

It's the difference in images I want to explore here. These images that the experts offer—the ones that go with "limits" and "testing"— have been valuable to me as a parent, so perhaps you will find them valuable too.

Limits come in two packages; physical and parental.

Physical limits are all the barriers and barricades you use to keep your children safe. They're the gates on the stairs in homes where toddlers live, locks on medicine cabinets, fences around swimming pools. You may have a rule to go along with these but you can rest assured that children are safe because they don't have a choice of whether or not to break the rule.

One example of a physical limit we use as a society is modern freeway design. You can't easily make a mistake. For example, there's no way to get on the off-ramp going the wrong way. The decision isn't yours; it was built into the design. You can't get across a well-designed center divider because a barricade stops you. We no longer depend on rules to keep us safe from wrong-way drivers, we protect them and us through physical limits.

As soon as you introduce restrictions to children, you discover the phenomenon called "testing." Adults don't need to check out the strength of the center divider but young children are less knowledgeable and need to test the physical limits they encounter. They jiggle the gate across the top of the stairs; they bang on the locked bathroom door. Usually they don't test long because they can see and feel physical limits. These kinds of restrictions are a physical fact. Children may express frustration when they bump up against these limits but once they discover the boundaries are solid, they eventually go about their business.

Parental limits—those restrictions or rules that we impose on our children for their own good and ours—are a different story. They aren't physical barricades that children can see and touch. They're more like an invisible fence. Children only come to know about this invisible fence when we tell or show them. In other words, their understanding of our limits comes from our words and behavior.

The only way children know exactly where these limits lie and how strong they are is by checking them out. They continually bump into our limits to discover the shape, size, and strength of the invisible fence.

They'll spend more time testing intangible parental limits than they will shaking a gate keeping them from the stairs. A good deal of misbehavior is the result of testing parental limits.

Here's an example of how testing parental limits works. The child throws a plastic toy across the room. The parent explains gently, but firmly, that it's not okay to throw toys. The child decides to test the limit to see if it really holds. She says to herself, "Does she really mean that?" She retrieves the toy and throws it again, noting the response. Then she asks herself, "If I drop the toy straight down on the floor—will she stop me?" She tries it and notes the response. Then she asks, "Can I throw some toys but not others?" She picks up a foam ball, throws it, and notes the response. "What if she's not looking—will I be stopped from throwing?" She waits until her mother's back is turned, then throws a doll and notes the response. This testing may not all occur at the same time and it is not always conscious but it is very real. This child is not being bad. She's testing.

Testing stops when children discover just how far they can go. They don't need to keep checking anymore once they discover where the invisible fence lies. Of course, that's only a temporary situation because as they grow and develop, their world expands and parental limits change to go along with their new abilities. They continually have a whole new set of boundaries to check out, which means the testing of parental limits doesn't end until the day they become the setters of their own limits.

26

DAWDLING

Some children take forever to do anything. You can't get them to get ready in the morning; to come to dinner at night; to get in or out of the bathtub.

There might be a number of reasons for this behavior but one that comes to mind first is problems with transitions. As a person with a transition problem, I understand children who dawdle perfectly.

For example, it has taken me a lifetime to even begin to enjoy getting up in the morning. I also don't look forward to going to bed at night. I hate getting ready for a vacation and have difficulty getting back to my normal life when vacation is over. In other words, I have trouble getting started and I have trouble stopping. I'm not good at transitions.

Even my birth reflects this theme of resisting change; I put off being born as long as I could. Two weeks past the due date, I finally made my entry into the world. Talk about dragging your feet! Fortunately, I didn't have a choice and was eventually pushed into the world, crying my head off.

I've quit crying now but I still struggle with change: letting go of a relationship; moving; leaving one job for another. Those are big changes and, like most people, I find them painful. But I also suffer over little daily transitions. Even getting up from the table when I'm through eating is something I put off doing.

Of course, even people with transition difficulties can be motivated to take the next step when that step brings them to something especially desired. I never used to have trouble getting up on Christmas morning, for example. However, most of life doesn't hold something wonderful at the next step.

So, how can you help children cope with transitions? Here are four suggestions:

• Don't push or prod—this creates resistance. Understand that it takes some children longer and that transitions cause unhappiness. Try to accept that fact. If you're a person who moves quickly through transitions without any difficult feelings, it may be very hard for you to understand someone who doesn't.

• Create a consistent routine. One thing automatically following another helps me and works for many children too. It's a matter of creating patterns and developing habits. For instance, when my son (who is like me) was little, I had a choice of sending him to preschool every day or for three days a week. Although I was home the extra two days, I chose to put him in all five days so that he experienced a consistent routine. This plan worked for us. He got used to the transition of going to school and coming home because every weekday was the same.

• Prepare your child for transitions by letting him know before they occur. For example, give warnings before leaving for school and ask the teachers to do the same at the end of the day.

• Allow plenty of time for transitions but don't be too upset if that doesn't always work. In my case, resistance to a change of activity lasts exactly as long as the time I have to resist. The time available for getting ready is the time I take. Getting me started sooner doesn't get rid of my dawdling; it just prolongs it. I tend to arrive places a little late because I never leave until I absolutely have to. I drive some people crazy—they're the ones who don't have transition problems.

I know a lot of little kids with transition problems like mine. You can fight them or you can handle them with patience and understanding. I advocate the latter.

_____ **27** _____

MAKING MESSES

How do you get children to pick up after themselves? Here are some simple guidelines:

• Make it easy for them to know where things go. That old saying, "a place for everything and everything in it's place" is a good rule to go by. Children develop a sense of order when they live in an organized environment.

• Make clean-up time fun. Young children can be enticed into thinking they're playing a game rather than doing a dreaded chore. If they have that attitude when they're young, they may grow up without knowing the difference.

• If the time should come when they don't regard clean-up as fun, take a problem-solving approach. Avoid power struggles. Discuss, negotiate, and figure out together how to restore order.

• Model orderliness by picking up after yourself. It's amazing how well children imitate what they see.

Simple. Just four guidelines and your problems are over, right? Wrong! If it's so easy, why is it that if you came over to my house to visit, you'd be likely to find a mess? Writing guidelines is easy; following them is the hard part. Knowing something and doing it are different things.

Where I fall down is in modeling. I'd like to finish and put away one project before I start another but I don't. Sometimes, one is a long-term project and another calls for my immediate attention.

Since I'm tolerant of myself, what can I say to a child who is in the middle of building a huge block structure when he suddenly decides he needs to go out and ride his bike for awhile? I can understand that need. I also understand that he's still working on the block structure. I let him go. Order suffers.

I also have a problem with a place for everything. If new possessions didn't keep arriving or if the old ones self-destructed, it wouldn't be so hard. But organizing and reorganizing takes time. I always have so many more pressing and interesting things to do than clean out closets and cupboards.

I also have trouble making clean-up time fun, since I'm often a grouch about it myself (just as my mother and her mother before her). My kids can pick up a true attitude in a minute, even when I'm pretending something is a fun little game.

I don't have trouble with problem-solving, negotiating, or figuring out a solution to get the place picked up when there's a real need. At those times, there's a real sense of urgency and the energy behind that gets me looking for the cooperation I need to make things happen. So we do have periods of real order at home. You **can** come over and find the place cleaned and tidy—**just be sure to let me know when you're coming!**

28

STUBBORNNESS

Stubborn behavior is normal.
Persistent individuals serve society well.

Photo credit: Frank Gonzalez-Mena

Some of the greatest achievements to humankind have come from strong-willed people who were brave enough to take a stand on what they believed. It's easy to appreciate persistence when it resides in an historical figure. Living with a stubborn child is a different matter.

The problem is that children can be stubborn about every little thing. They aren't able to sort out the important issues from the minor ones. They also don't always know what is best for them and they can seldom put the needs of others before their own. Once they learn all that, stubbornness can be a valuable trait.

In the meantime, though, a persistent child can be a tremendous headache. There are some ways to make life easier for all while you're waiting for the stubbornness to become an asset. Here are some ideas about getting along with a persistent child and simultaneously promoting cooperation:

• Teach cooperation by modeling it. If you are often stubborn and demanding yourself, rather than cooperative, you won't be an effective teacher.

• Try not to issue challenges. You have a better chance for cooperation if you make a positive statement rather than give out orders. Say, "Feet belong on the floor not on the couch," rather than "Get your feet off the couch right now!" or even "Please put your feet down." If you use the right tone of voice, one that is matter-of-fact and not at all challenging, the child may respond instead of resisting.

• Avoid all unnecessary demands. Don't ask your child to do something that you're not prepared to carry through on. If you wish he would do something but don't absolutely require it, give a choice. Children with choices are less likely to be stubborn. Example: "I'd really like you to come in now and wash your hands for lunch but if you're not ready to eat just yet you can play in the back yard a little longer." Then, if you discover it's the handwashing he's resisting, give more choices. "Do you want to wash your hands in the sink or the bathroom?"

• When you do make an absolutely necessary demand, be very clear about what you expect and be prepared to insist. "You may not throw your little cars. I will stop you if you can't stop yourself."

• Once you've enforced a demand, let your child express his displeasure but don't let the protests get to you. If you give a lot of attention to protests, you teach children that they can gain attention through fussing. Acknowledge the feelings briefly with something like, "I know you're unhappy that I put the little cars away..."

- Don't allow children to manipulate you with their protests. If you give in to their refusal to do something that you've decided is absolutely necessary, you are teaching them that if they make a big enough fuss they can get their way. (Just be careful you don't find too many things **absolutely necessary** for them to do. When you make demands only rarely, then you can put your all into handling the refusal.)

- Avoid using fear to rule—this approach will not teach true cooperation. Cooperation is a spirit, an attitude behind a behavior, not the behavior itself. Replace threats and punishments with gentle, persistent firmness. Threatened or punished children often become less cooperative and even more obstinate.

It helps to recognize that stubborn behavior is normal. Obstinacy occurs naturally when children are thwarted, yet they must learn to accept other people's ways and wishes, as well as control their own. This won't happen overnight—in fact, it takes some people years. We have to be very patient.

Of course, it's easier to be around children who are always cooperative and compliant but is that your only goal? After all, you want your children to use their own heads; to make their own decisions; to question now and then; and when they're sure they're right, to persevere. Persistence is a good character trait and will take your child a long way once he learns the benefits of cooperation.

V

SELF-ESTEEM

Developing self-esteem is a life-long
process linked with the search for identity.

Photo credit: Jim Darter

29

TRYING TO PROGRAM CHILDREN FOR HIGH SELF-ESTEEM

Can you program a child for high self-esteem? Some people think so but a child is not a computer. You can control input to some extent (perhaps) but you can't control output. You can send messages, although you have no guarantee as to how they will be received.

Take the simple message "I love you." Self-esteem, for most of us, depends to a varying extent on our perception of our lovableness—or perhaps significance is a better word. With that in mind, we tell our children we love them. To add power, we couple the words with nonverbal messages like hugs and kisses. Since we also perform other ongoing loving behaviors such as feeding, clothing, and meeting other needs, we think that we can sit back, assured that our children are loved. Perhaps they are loved but do they **feel** loved?

There are no guarantees. We can input all we want, but unlike computers who merely **receive** input, children **perceive** input and they do so in a variety of unpredictable ways. We have no control over those perceptions. The point is, children who are loved don't necessarily **feel** loved.

Programming for high self-esteem is a simplistic approach. I'm not saying parents shouldn't tell their children they love them or give them plenty of hugs and kisses. I'm just saying that the messages alone won't insure high self-esteem.

Let's look at some other areas besides significance that are linked with self-esteem. To varying degrees, most of us also depend on our perception of our competence, virtue, and power to determine how we feel about ourselves. For this to be a valid measure, (rather than the product of a delusional mind) we must do some kind of reality check. My favorite definition of high self-esteem goes something like this—if an honest and realistic self-assessment of strengths and weaknesses results in more pluses than minuses, you have high self-esteem.

This self-assessment isn't something you sit down and do as an exercise for a class on personal development. This is a life-long process linked with the search for identity. It starts in infancy and continues, mostly on the unconscious level, throughout life as you ask yourself who you are and supply yourself with the answers. This is a process that involves choices—both conscious and unconscious. It's the element of choice that makes us different from computers.

At this point in history, we know a lot more about lowering self-esteem than we do about raising it. We know what not to do. That's where the programming idea comes in. Since negative input tears down self-esteem, it seems logical that reversing the process would build it up. But it isn't that simple. If it was, parenting would be a cinch!

So what is a parent to do? Here's my advice. While continuing to give your children positive input, concentrate the rest of your effort into working on your own self-esteem. Children's self-esteem is linked to their parents' self-esteem. Even without research, that's pretty easy to see.

You can't control your children's choices or perceptions but you can make some decisions about your own. Start by deciding if your self-esteem needs to be boosted or if you're okay the way you are. If you're ready to upgrade, start by discovering which of the four areas are the most important to your own sense of self-worth—significance, competence, virtue, or power. Concentrate on the important area. For example, if you find yourself loveable but powerless, go to work on learning about your power and how to use it. Perhaps you could take an assertiveness-training class.

Eventually, you'll be able answer the question "Who am I?" with a positive response; and know that by doing so there's a chance your children will too.

30

PLEASING PEOPLE

I was a people-pleasing child. I felt good when others were happy and awful when they weren't. That put me under the control of others. My strings were in their hands.

Making decisions solely on the basis of what makes others happy is not a healthy way to live.

Looking back, I realize I was less concerned about doing what was best than I was about keeping out of trouble. I greatly feared the anger of others. My unconscious, childish reasoning went something like this, "If you're mad at me you may leave me; and I can't survive without you." We all have abandonment issues left from infancy. Some of us carry them with us as if we are still unable to survive on our own.

With these kinds of fears, even mild disapproval can be used to manipulate. I remember times when I clashed wills with someone. As soon as that person called me inconsiderate or selfish, I would immediately tune out my own needs and switch to trying to prove I was not selfish or inconsiderate.

I'd like to think that's all in the past but the truth is I'm still hooked on the approval of others. Pleasing others has been a way of life for me. Only with difficulty am I finding another way.

Why am I telling you all this? I'm telling you because if parents recognize that they or their children are in this pattern, they can do something about it.

It's worth trying to change because people-pleasers are less likely to understand their own needs. They have a narrow view of right and wrong. They lack the courage to follow their own sense of direction. They're less likely to be their own person and more likely to be the puppet of someone else.

How do parents hook kids on approval? One of the most powerful ways is withdrawal of love. When children grow up with conditional love—that is love which is dependent on pleasing the dominant adults in their lives—they lose touch with their ability to make decisions. They lose touch with their needs. They become dependent on pleasing others in order to keep their love.

Withdrawal of love may not be intended but children who aren't sure they are loved unconditionally sometimes get messages their parents don't mean to send. For example, if a parent continually criticizes people for being fat, a daughter who is putting on weight may question whether or not she is still loved.

Some children get labeled and then must live up to the label in order to continue to win approval. That was my problem. I was a good girl from the day I was born. I had a lot of unconscious investment in keeping my title and I worked hard at it throughout my childhood. I would have been a lot better off if my family had pointed out the **behaviors** that pleased them instead of giving me such a global label to live up to.

They thought this label would encourage me to keep being good—which it did. But it also encouraged me to define "good" by what made them happy, not by what I needed or by what was best. Sometimes what I needed conflicted with what the important adults in my life needed or wanted. In these circumstances, I tended to give in to please them.

To summarize, parents can unhook themselves and their children on approval by giving unconditional love. Focus on **behavior** without making judgments about the **worth** of the person. When adults and children quit people-pleasing, they make better decisions because they gain a sense of direction—their own feeling for what is right and wrong. Parents can help this process by tuning in to who they are and what their needs are; and encouraging their children to do the same. They can regard conflicts of needs as opportunities to explore win/win solutions so that neither they nor their children are always giving in.

———— 31 ————

AVOID MANIPULATIVE PRAISE

"Oh, honey, what a pretty picture!" gushes Jennifer about the black and yellow felt pen smears thrust in her face. She puts aside her magazine to hug the artist, her three-year-old daughter, Briana. "I love it!" she says with false enthusiasm, holding the torn piece of notebook paper at arm's length. "What an artist you are!" She hands back the sheet and returns to her magazine. The smile that never quite reached her eyes is still frozen on her lips as she starts reading again.

Jennifer wants to be left alone. She figures that her response will buy her some more time because she believes that praise motivates. Her idea is to keep her daughter drawing. Jennifer uses this technique all the time without analyzing its effects.

Respond to children's art by making
nonjudgmental observations rather
than gushing fake praise.

Photo credit: Robert Sturm

Jennifer has a reason for using praise; as a child she was
criticized a great deal. In this situation, her mother would have said,
"Quit interrupting me. Can't you see I'm busy? You're such a selfish
child."

It's a mild reproach, granted, but Jennifer remembers the sting.
She knows that criticism tears down self-esteem. She doesn't want
to control her daughter's behavior through criticism so she has
switched to praise. Her intent is to manipulate Briana's behavior
while preserving her self-esteem.

Does the manipulation work? Let's go back to the scene and see what happens next. Jennifer, buried again in her magazine, is just about to find out the secret of the diet plan that allows you to eat all your favorite foods. At the moment of revelation, Briana thrusts a second smeary drawing in her face. Faithful Jennifer puts down her magazine and again gushes and bubbles over the "picture."

Three minutes later, Briana reappears with yet another smear and they go through the same routine. This pattern continues with Briana spending less and less time on each picture and demanding more and more praise. Jennifer finally gives up and takes her out for a walk around the block.

What happened here? Why did Jennifer's approach backfire? She wasn't honest. She never acknowledged what was really going on. She wanted time alone and Briana wanted her attention. Those are the facts that were never put into words. Jennifer tried to manipulate her daughter instead of dealing with the true situation. Was Jennifer wrong in attempting to get time for herself? No. It's important for parents to take care of themselves. The problem was that she was never honest with Briana about what she needed.

Was she wrong in focusing on Briana's self-esteem? Of course not. Self-esteem is vital to development but it doesn't come from empty words. It comes when children experience legitimate successes and feel good about them. Briana was drawing for her mother, not for her own pleasure. Jennifer was pretending to be excited about pictures she didn't really admire.

What could Jennifer have done instead? She could have been honest. She could have told Briana that she wanted to be left alone right then. She could have conveyed her message without criticizing her daughter; or she could have taken the time to make nonjudgmental comments about some aspect of the picture or the process.

Statements like "I see you used more black than yellow" or "I bet you really enjoyed smearing the colors" are honest. They are a reflection of reality and more encouraging than a big fake "*Wow!*" over the picture itself.

Praise with a purpose is sneaky and manipulative. It's important to be above-board with our children—but even more importantly, we need to be straight with ourselves. We must admit when we are being manipulative. Once we acknowledge that we're behaving in dishonest and sneaky ways, we can quit. When we begin to give up manipulation in all its forms, including criticism **and** praise, we're on the path to healthy parenting.

32

BALANCING SKILLS IS IMPORTANT

Children need to learn both leading and following skills. Some children are born with natural tendencies toward one role or the other but they need to balance those natural tendencies with some experiences on the other side. How do they get these experiences? They get them from you.

Today, I went on a hike with my husband. We fell into our old patterns. On a hike, he is the leader. Every now and then, we switch roles and I lead. But inevitably, he takes over the lead the first time I take a direction of which he doesn't approve. This happens so automatically, we never even think about it. We don't discuss it or even recognize it is happening. It's an unconscious pattern.

My advice is to look out for these kinds of patterns in your life, especially when you're with your children. How often do you take the lead and the child follows along?

Try switching roles. If you usually lead, let your child lead. Of course, that doesn't mean you have to be completely passive. Followers can give suggestions and advice to the leaders—it's not that parents who are being led give up their protector role or abdicate all responsibility. Letting a child lead gives that child a chance to experience the leader role.

This leader/follower theme is especially clear when I think back to all the museums I've taken my children to. Actually, it's not only museums, it's wherever we've gone that I expected my children to have an educational experience. I almost always took the lead. I would start by making the plan, then I'd herd everybody around so they saw all the things I thought were important. I did take individual considerations into account but I clearly was the leader.

Once I realized it didn't have to be this way, things changed. I remember the time we went to visit an Early California Mission which, of course, was to be an educational experience. Although we skipped the tour, I found myself conducting my own. Suddenly I realized what I was doing—what kinds of expectations I had for this experience. I decided to try letting go. I put the children in charge and followed them around. It was hard when they skipped things I thought were important and dwelt on things I thought weren't, but I managed to keep from taking charge. We saw very different aspects of the mission than what I had expected. However, I must say it was not only educational but interesting for all of us. In fact, I had to drag the children out—not the usual ending of an educational experience.

The time that it is easiest to see this principle at work is when you take a toddler for a walk. If you have your own plan that involves a goal of getting somewhere in some specific period of time, you'd better take a stroller or carry the child. The whole complexion of the walk changes when you relax and let the child take the lead. If you and the toddler were to leave a trail like a snail does, looking back on it you'd find that it goes in loops and spirals; recrossing itself, backtracking, sidetracking, and every-which-way-tracking. There is nothing linear about a walk with a toddler. That's the way toddlers walk. You can too, if you get out of a goal-oriented leadership role and into a receptive follower role.

So next time you find yourself initiating things in a take-charge kind of way, think about the possibility of changing things around and giving your child a chance to learn some leadership skills.

33

ENCOURAGING COMPETENCE

Developing competence is an important goal—
one that brings self-esteem, power and self-control.

Photo credit: Cris Evans

I remember the day my son, Timmy, fixed us all lunch for the first time. He made Mexican pizza in the microwave; using flour tortillas, pizza sauce, and grated cheese. I remember the scene well. From where I was sitting in the other room, I could just see the top of his Giant's hat over the counter. It was moving quickly back and forth across the kitchen. I'm not sure why this recipe caused so much movement but he certainly created a lot while putting the ingredients together.

"This is a big moment in my life!" he exclaimed, stopping in his path for a moment, cheese grater in hand, to share his pleasure with me. I agreed. Then I responded, "I remember the last meal you fixed for us—Cheerios in bed one rainy morning. Remember?" "Yes," he grinned. Then he grinned even broader—"But this is a lot more high tech!"

I had to admit it was. He's growing in his abilities and his competencies. And he feels good about that fact.

How often do we keep our children from gaining competency and feeling good because we do things for them? I'm guilty—so I'm assuming you are too, at least occasionally.

What keeps us from encouraging competence?

● Perfectionist tendencies. All parents have been faced with the problem of deciding whether to encourage a child to do something or just do it themselves so it will be done right. I remember all the bed-making episodes with my daughter who was so anxious to help but much too young to make a bed to my standards. I was always so tempted to put the finishing touches on. If I yielded to the temptation, it always hurt her feelings.

● Lack of time. Sometimes the issue isn't standards but time pressures. How hard it is, when you're late in the morning, to wait with patience to let children finish what they need to do. "Here, I'll tie your shoes today—we're late!"

● Lack of expectations. We usually start parenthood with relatively helpless babies and we get used to the idea that they need to have everything done for them. It takes some parents longer than others to get out of that mindset as their children develop capabilities little by little.

● Need to nurture. Some parents have an overdeveloped need to nurture. They want to keep their children small and take care of every little need and want. Or perhaps it's just the last child they treat this way. Grandparents have been known to have this problem, too.

Developing competence is an important life goal—one that brings with it self-esteem, power, and self-control. I try to remember that as I live day-to-day with my children.

34

EMPOWERING CHILDREN

What does it mean to empower someone? To empower means to enable someone to experience his or her own power. What does "power" mean? Although obviously related to energy, vigor, and strength, the word is often narrowly used in the sense of domination or control. I am speaking of a different kind of energy—one more in tune with the original root meaning of the word which is "to be able."

"To be able" implies effectiveness and competence, which I take to mean the ability to behave in ways that meet needs. This ability gives people freedom to reflect to the world who they truly are. None of these definitions necessarily include dominating other people.

As parents, it is our job to empower our children. Here are five ways to do that:

- Set up an environment that makes children increasingly less dependent on you. A simple example is to put things they need and use in reach so they can get them themselves.
- Give them choices and opportunities to solve problems. Make sure they experience decision-making.
- Build security. If they learn to trust you and their environment, they begin to experience their own power. If they live in an inconsistent world where predictability is impossible, they will feel powerless.
- Make them feel important and significant, as well as loved. Let them know they matter to you and to others.
- Help them feel virtuous. That's not hard if the child has the natural ability to make people happy or is a people-pleaser.

You'll barely have to work at it. Children lose their sense of virtue when parents hammer away at the child's badness; point out faults; constantly focus on weaknesses.

In summary, you help children experience personal power— that is, their ability to meet their needs; to become who they really are—by helping them see themselves as competent, virtuous, significant, and loveable.

By overpowering your children and always keeping them in your control, you teach them that domination is the only kind of power. Further, if they feel incompetent, insignificant, or lack virtue; you always have to be on guard so they don't hurt you or someone else to prove it. You have to be mighty careful that their behavior is under outside control—yours or someone else's—at all times.

Dominated children tend to grow up less than whole and healthy people. **And** you have to constantly worry that they'll grow strong enough to overpower **you**. Further, if you succeeded in dominating without giving them a sense of virtue and lovableness, they may find significance through despicable behavior. History gives us evidence that such a thing can happen. We can all name significant tyrants and vicious villains, both modern and ancient. They live in our memories. Yet what isn't part of our memories is that these despicable people came from disempowering, abusive childhoods.

So it is worth empowering the children in our lives for our own benefit as well as theirs. I hope I have convinced you. Most of us were raised in a less than empowering way. The old-fashioned way of child-rearing was to squelch power; break wills; ignore needs. It's a vicious cycle that continues until someone consciously breaks it. My aim is to change things. How about you?

VI

KIDS ARE INDIVIDUALS

Some children are product people—
others are more interested in process.

Photo credit: Robert Sturm

35

THE BOY WHO DESTROYED EVERYTHING HE EVER MADE

Some kids start weeks ahead of time on school projects. My son, before he became more responsible, used to start about five minutes to bedtime the night before the project was due. His approach was to work frantically to get his parents to produce the thing. He's better now but he still dislikes projects.

Tim's last completely self-initiated project was in second grade when, on his own, he produced an amazing crumpled paper and aluminum foil volcano for the science fair. It took him about fifteen minutes and two rolls of scotch tape. He was proud when he finished but when he was done—he was done. He didn't want to hear that a science fair entry needed something more than just one volcano. "You have to answer a question," I told him. Finally, just before the bus arrived, he came up with, "What happens when you hit lava rock with a hammer?" which he hastily scrawled on the base of the volcano. He had just enough time to whack some lava rock from the back yard with a hammer and glue the results of the experiment to the volcano when the bus pulled up. He climbed aboard trailing tape and dripping glue.

The best part of the project was not in the making nor in the ribbon he won. What he really enjoyed was bringing the volcano home, setting fire to the whole thing and watching it go up in smoke. The look of joy on his face was the same one he gets when he demolishes a sand castle that he has spent a whole day at the beach building.

It used to bug me that my child was like this—never producing anything he regarded as worthy of preserving. I wanted him to be more like his friend, Paul, who is always making something worth keeping. Even Paul's bug collection, instead of being strewn under his bed, is neatly displayed on boards; each specimen carefully labeled. Paul is a producer.

Now, I don't believe in comparing one child to another but deep down I used to wish Tim would be a producer too. It was a big step for me to realize that he's fine just as he is. He doesn't need a **product** to be happy. He needs an **experience**.

I think back to the years when Tim's major occupation was either running around outside "pretending" or playing inside with action figures. He almost never **made things** unless he was producing a setting for his play. For example, he built block structures but he didn't value them for themselves—only as they contributed to the action play. He knocked them over as easily as he built them.

Tim outgrew this kind of play and began to spend his free time outside skateboarding day and night. One cold and windy evening he quit skating early. "Where's some cardboard?" he asked me. I told him. I was surprised to see him a little later with cardboard, scissors, glue, and tape in hand; disappearing into his room. That's something he never does—the last time was five years ago when he produced that science fair volcano. Was he working on some kind of project?

I peeked in a little later. There he sat among a pile of cardboard scraps and discarded rolls of tape; surrounded by miniature ramps, rail slides, spines, and other structures skateboarders risk their bones on. In his hand was a tiny skateboard. "I'm skating my fingerboard," he announced.

It's said that the world is divided into two kinds of people—those that divide the world into two kinds of people and those that don't. I'm the former. And I've just divided the world into "process people" and "product people." Look around you—you'll see this division works. I know a process man who works hard all year long just so he can spend his money climbing a major mountain of the world on his vacation. He puts out extraordinary effort and expense in these climbs, yet he has nothing to show for it.

I notice the trend is to value process people more. Some people have even figured out how to make a buck on them by selling them "adventure packages." Even ordinary people go on treks to Patagonia to bring back nothing but windburn. (This is very different from the rich hunters who used to go to Africa to collect trophies.)

I have to admit I'm more of a product person. I enjoy process but I want a product too, and once I finish something, I never destroy it. I don't want to go to Patagonia to collect windburn. I'd never burn my paper volcano. Now that I've thought about it, though, I can appreciate someone who does.

36

IT TAKES ALL TYPES

Allow the dreamer to dream on, the
dancer to dance, and the artist to paint.

Photo credit: Unknown

Some children are object-focused, while some are more interested
in **people** than they are **things**. They use objects but they use them
to enhance the social world they love so much. In nursery school or
the day care center, you'll find these children who are more oriented
to others offering pretend cups of coffee to playmates or singing to
dolls. They may have turned the playhouse area into a spaceship and
are busy practicing people skills on their way to Mars. These
children use **things** but it's **people** and **human relations** that most
intrigue them. They show an intense interest in learning about others;
in interpreting messages; in reading feelings. They practice these
skills every day.

The object-oriented child, in exactly the same environment, will ignore the cups of coffee, the dolls, and the spaceship relationships but instead will be under the table with some kind of tool trying to unbolt the legs. I remember an object-oriented child who was given a jumble of padlocks and keys that had been collecting in the preschool cupboard for years. This child, who seldom sat still for five minutes during circle time, spent an entire hour matching up locks and keys—an enormous task that no teacher at the center had been willing to tackle.

This same child told me a year or two later, when I was trying to take the training wheels off his bike, that I needed to turn the nuts the opposite way I was turning them. (Not being an object person myself, I never have paid attention to little physical details like that.)

Not all individuals focus mainly on people or objects. A third group is "self-oriented." They have an inward focus. They are their own central interest. The "self-oriented" child is the one you see in the nursery school or day care center off by herself swinging dreamily on the hammock or painting for long periods at the easel. These children often worry preschool teachers. They seem preoccupied; disengaged. The urgency is to get them involved—to busy them with either people or objects.

My message is to celebrate differences by allowing children their individuality. At the same time, provide each child with a variety of experiences to improve the balance of the different aspects of each personality. Allow the dreamer to dream on; the dancer to dance; the artist to paint; but also encourage relationships with other people, as well as some experience with objects in the environment. Allow the budding mechanic to practice her skills but get her involved with people also. Help her get in touch with herself. Encourage the relationships expert to at least take a look at the broken tricycle and do some speculating about how to fix it. Maybe he'll learn which way to unscrew a bolt before I did.

Of course, no child is all one way or the other—most are a combination. Think about the adult population and early orientation—can you see that engineers, mechanics, and physicists were probably object-oriented children? Those people you know in the service professions were probably people-oriented as far back as toddlerhood.

Then there are the artists, dancers, and writers. The tendency for self-absorption comes early in some of these types. I've noticed that sometimes, even in infants, you can tell one type from the other. Some babies are focused inwardly and others focus more outside themselves.

Where do you fit in the "object," "other-people," and "self-oriented" categories? Are you more one type than the other? Where do your children fit? Do your differences complement or conflict with each other?

_____ **37** _____

THE ANGEL/DEVIL SYNDROME

Some children are very hard to get along with. That's no news to some of you. What may be news is that some of those same little devils are angels when they're not at home. I'll tell you about such a child.

This child tended to be rude, crude, grouchy, and moody; at least from the viewpoint of the parent. I don't believe in labels or name-calling, so I have to stop giving you descriptive words but I think you have the picture. This child was very hard to be around.

When this child's parents met up with his friends' parents they got a different picture. Guess what the friends' parents would say. "Your child is so polite, kind, and considerate; a real pleasure to have around." Surprise!

Why would a child be so different at home? Is this the old split personality phenomenon? No. The explanation has nothing to do with mental illness, it has to do with the child's personality and the way he or she is raised.

Some children have a basic sense of security that allows them to be themselves wherever they are. They express their feelings to whomever is around—strangers, acquaintances, friends, relatives, and parents. Other children feel less secure and trusting in the outside world. They are the ones who are more likely to bestow the pleasant parts of their personality on outsiders, leaving the less pleasant parts for home.

It works something like this. At home, the consequences of crudeness, rudeness, and a variety of ways of expressing anger are already tested. Outside the home, it is usually less clear what happens to you if you grouch, complain, throw a fit or make a rude remark. Many children are not willing to find out. Instead, they gather up their energy to put on a good face when they are away from home.

Fine. Why can't they put on a good face at home too? It's a matter of resources. It takes a lot of energy to suppress feelings. The child arrives at home with reserves exhausted. The expression "to let down one's hair" fits perfectly here. When the hair comes down, the first thing to go is the mannerly veneer. Home is where it is safe to vent pent-up rage, annoyance, and disgust.

Of course, children can express feelings without being crude, rude, having fits or being grouchy; but they have to learn how. They won't learn in a family where any expression of anger may be considered rude.

Children who have been taught that anger is something to be avoided try to hide their feelings. Stuffing feelings takes a lot of effort. After a period of holding in your true feelings, you begin to let down your guard. If home is a safe place, when you get there, the feelings spill out all over.

Another factor in the angel/devil child is people-pleasing, which is taught in the name of manners, kindness, and consideration. People-pleasing is often an away-from-home phenomenon, so that by the time children get home they have already done their quota of pleasing for the day. When they stop pleasing outsiders and start pleasing themselves, most put little thought into the effect they have on those at the home front.

So what can you do if you live with children who are hard to get along with? Teach them to express anger appropriately, both at home and abroad. Help them see that anger is not bad but is merely a feeling that can be used to rally energy resources for problem-solving. Teach true kindness and consideration rather than surface manners and simplistic people-pleasing. (Modeling is the best way to teach these.)

And take a look at yourself. What are you like when you're in the bigger world? What are you like at home? Are you setting a good example?

38

CONTRARY CHILDREN

Some children put a lot of focus into people-pleasing. They are often labeled a "good child." Other children are exactly the opposite—they go out of their way *not* to please people. They are often labeled a "bad child."

Sometimes both of these kinds of children end up in the same family; it is no coincidence that they are opposites. They are a contrast to each other because they are striving for their identity—their individuality. Instead of being who they really are, they define themselves in reaction to a sibling. A common pattern is for the good child to be the first child. The second child, at some point, decides not to compete for the title of best child so he or she becomes the worst child. This pattern can also be reversed when the second child is "good" in reaction to an older sibling's "bad" behavior.

What are the payoffs for the "bad child"? Why would a child spend a lifetime making parents miserable? Besides creating a personality and an approach to life distinctive from a sibling, "bad children" get lots of attention. They take a good deal of parental energy and focus as the adults keep reacting to the behavior and trying to change it. They usually get more attention than good children, who are so busy not making waves that they sometimes get ignored.

Power may be an issue with a misbehaving child. Nothing is more powerful than creating havoc in everyone's lives. Knowing how to stir things up gives a child a sense of control. Making people happy is less dramatic and to a confirmed, contrary child, may feel like selling out.

Contrary children, like their people-pleasing counterparts, lack freedom because they only **react** to others. Neither type of child is in touch with needs.

Now while no one is trying to change the behavior of the people-pleasing child, everyone is concerned about the contrary child. Here are some hints about how to help "bad children" misbehave less:

- Get rid of labels. Don't classify. Don't let children push you into categorizing them as "good" or "bad."
- Lighten up. If the payoff for the child is attention, withdrawing it for bad behavior removes the reason the behavior exists in the first place. The problem is that all children need attention and if misbehavior is the way they are used to getting it, you'll be hard pressed to find ways to give attention for good behavior. But that's what you must do. Catch them being good every single chance you can.
- Work on power issues and self-esteem. It won't be easy if the child is already in a strong pattern but it's worth working on. One way to help children feel more powerful is to give them choices. You don't have to offer a whole world of options. Limit the choices to a couple of alternatives.
- Don't ever compare them to other children, especially to siblings. You want them to see themselves as unique individuals. The competitions children create and parents fan the flames of, contribute greatly to decisions children make about their behavior.

I don't mean to downplay the difficulty of changing the behavior of a confirmed, contrary child. If you have a child like this, you know it isn't easy. But if you look at all the child is missing out on—freedom to be who he or she really is; pleasure from positive relationships; ability to meet needs—you'll see it's worth trying to make some changes. Besides, think of how much better **your** life will be when your child quits making your displeasure his or her primary goal!

—————— **39** ——————

DIFFICULT CHILDREN

Contrary children find power, satisfaction, and their identity by creating havoc in family life. *Difficult children*, on the other hand, are those children who misbehave because their needs conflict with their parents' needs.

Though both contrary children and difficult children may misbehave frequently, the goal behind their misbehavior differs.

Contrary children seek to displease others, regardless of their own needs. The goal of difficult children is to meet their own needs even if they have to misbehave.

Let me describe a difficult child to you. This child was highly active from the day he was born. Always on the move, he often got in trouble because of his insatiable curiosity about the world and everything in it. He couldn't keep his hands off things. They called to him to be explored, manipulated, and even taken apart. This often resulted in their destruction, much to the chagrin of the adults in this child's life. Limits were set but the lure of curiosity was too strong to keep this child within those limits.

This child also experienced intense distress when basic needs called him. For example, when he was hungry, he couldn't wait. When he needed to move his body there was no restraining him.

School was a nightmare for this child because it required him to sit quietly for a long time. Needs were expected to be put on hold until recess. His mind was as quick as his hands. He was extremely impatient with lengthy tasks that required him to slow down his own learning process in order to practice skills the teacher deemed necessary.

This child was driven. He was fascinated with those things that caught his interest and could spend long hours of concentration on them. Everything else got only fleeting attention. When he wasn't interested he became restless, impatient, and disobedient. He had a hard time controlling urges.

Pleasing or displeasing people did not concern him. Sometimes he was surprised at how irritated people were with him but their irritation did no more to motivate his behavior than did their pleasure.

Difficult children are not trying to live up to a title, they are merely acting on strong inner needs. They get along best with people who understand their motives and appreciate their intensity without trying to change them. They don't fit easily into anyone's mold.

If your child is a *difficult child*, you can:

- Recognize when misbehavior is a result of conflicting needs and bring that fact out in the open. Don't think of your child as bad, think of him or her as needy.

- Work on your problem-solving skills. You can put your needs first but be clear about how and why you are prioritizing. Help your child learn to predict what decisions you make about whose needs come first in which situations. Help your child have a part in those decisions.

• Look out for power struggles and avoid them. Your decision to put your own needs first, when that is appropriate, may trigger a battle. Find ways you can both be winners or avoid the battles altogether.

• Work on self-esteem. Being in constant conflict with others may wear down the child's sense of self-worth. Help your child find value by regarding him or her in a positive light.

If you weren't a difficult child yourself, you may have a hard time understanding how anyone could be so intense about getting needs met. You don't have to understand—just respect that your child is different from you. Then put your energy into figuring out how the two of you can get along and both get your needs met!

40

TAMING THE WILD CHILD

Wildness can come from many sources. What you do about it depends on what's causing it. Take a five-year-old boy who is continually on the move, destructive, and generally disregards limits. What might be going on with him?

Perhaps this child has an overabundance of energy and is in an environment where he can't use it. There's nothing like a sufficient amount of physical exercise to wear a child out. Children who spend most of their time outdoors running, climbing, digging, exploring, and discovering other ways to use their bodies fall into bed tired at night. They need less taming than those who spend their days inside with people telling them to settle down and be quiet.

Compare a pet cat who has plenty of opportunities to be outside to a lion at the zoo. The cat manages to settle down quite well when in the house. If she can't, you can put her outside. The lion paces endlessly because she never gets to do what she needs to—roam freely using her body the way it was designed to be used.

Over-stimulation can also cause children to be wild. One of the tasks of the young child is to learn to screen out excess sight, sound, and other kinds of stimulation. Some children are skilled screeners and others, for whatever reason, are unable to select particular things to focus on. They can't ignore all the other things coming in through their senses.

A child in a classroom of other children provides an example of this problem. Thirty children in one small space can be a very stimulating experience for someone who doesn't know how to focus attention. Think of the riot of color, movement, and small noises, even if the children are quiet. Most difficult of all, for some sensitive children, are what might be thought of as vibrations. Unconscious and conscious nonverbal communication is always going on when people are together. Some children pick up all these messages—too many for them to handle. The result is over-stimulation, which drives them wild. Until they learn screening skills, they'll benefit from being in an environment that doesn't overwhelm them.

Diet may contribute to wildness. The research is not absolutely clear on how food affects behavior. Certainly, we are all controlled by our body chemistry. That's bound to be influenced to a greater or lesser extent by what we eat. Food sensitivities may contribute to behavior problems.

Emotions could be another source of wildness. Children store their feelings until they build up. If you boil water in a sealed pot, like a pressure cooker, it builds steam until it reaches a point where the whole thing blows. Children are like that. Some continually blow up just to ease the unbearable pressure. They're wild. They need to learn ways to let off steam without hurting anyone. Talking about feelings can help. Engaging in calm, soothing activities can also help. One time-honored device is water. Water play can calm a wild child in no time at all. Baths may work, too.

Sometimes a child is wild because he has learned it's a sure way to get attention. If the behavior is learned, it's necessary to unlearn it. The child must be taught other ways to get attention; that means someone must lavish attention whenever the child is not being wild. At the same time, the wildness must be ignored as much as possible when it occurs. That's very hard to do if the child is destructive. It helps if the parent understands the principles of behavior modification, a method of changing behavior that has carefully delineated steps.

Whatever approach you use to tame a wild child, it is absolutely necessary that he not be allowed to hurt anything or anybody,

84

including himself. For some children, that means constant vigilance until they can be absolutely trusted. It's a full-time job and not an easy one!

VII

A FEW LAUGHS

Look who's laughing.

Photo credit: Paul Wallach

THE NIGHT WE ALL WORE BIBS TO DINNER

One of my babies refused to wear a bib as soon as he was old enough to protest. Whenever I put one on him he put up a fight, tearing and snatching at the thing around his throat in such obvious agony that I would decide it just wasn't worth it. After all, it isn't that much harder to wash a little shirt than it is to wash a bib. So I gave up on bibs—that is until the night of his first spaghetti dinner.

When I sat him down at the table, I had visions of permanent spaghetti stains on his sweet little shirt. I was in a no-nonsense mood so I didn't consider changing the shirt. I just got a bib and proceeded to try to put it on him. He protested as he always had.

"Well," I said to myself. "This time I'm going to get my way." I tried sweet-talking him—no go. Inspired with a clever idea, I got out his supply of bibs and put one on each of us. What a picture we all made, sitting at the dinner table with our baby bibs around our necks. I cheerily showed him how everybody had a bib on and then held up one for him—he grabbed it out of my hand and threw it on the floor.

That did it. I'd reached the end of my rope. I did something I seldom do to my children; I forced him. It took two of us to get the bib on him. Once it was snapped, he couldn't pull it off, though he continued to try.

Dinner was a miserable affair—my bibbed baby refused to eat a bite. But now I was in this you'll-do-as-I-say mood and I just couldn't let go. I harped at him. It wasn't until I resorted to trying to spoon feed him that he came to the end of his rope too.

I tried to poke the spoon into his mouth; he clamped it shut. I tried to distract him and slip the spoon in when he wasn't looking. I can feel my face flushing just putting this on paper. Then I turned to another family member who was asking me to pass the salad. That was when my innocent baby picked up his plate of spaghetti and... when I turned back, spoon in hand, he let me have it—the full plate—right in the face.

I have selective amnesia whenever I try to recall my immediate reaction to an event as dramatic as this one. I honestly don't remember what I did. To tell you the truth, I don't even know what I should have done. What would a child development expert advise once a parent had let things go this far? I don't know.

What I do remember is that the whole thing was over once the spaghetti hit the fan (so to speak). By the time the mess was cleaned up, the air was completely cleared. The tension was gone and so were the bibs—all of them—permanently. The only reminder was the big spaghetti stain on my blouse.

I learned a couple of lessons from this experience. Since I was miserably sweaty under the plastic backing of the bib, I finally understood my son's objections. I never saw his point of view before—I just thought he was being stubborn.

I also learned not to let things get out of hand like that. It was a good lesson—one I won't forget. I've kept my stained blouse as a reminder.

42

CHILDREN ENTER WHERE ADULTS FEAR TO TREAD

I remember an early encounter I had with computers back when I was still afraid of them. It was a long time ago in a mall. A crowd was gathered around a flickering screen in a computer store. I was at the back of the crowd and couldn't see what was going on. My son, Adam, who had never touched a computer in his life, wiggled his way up to the front of the crowd. When the man who was punching in things on the keyboard gave up and wandered off, Adam stepped forward and took his place. By then I was close enough to see what was happening.

Adam read the question on the screen—"What's your name?" Although he wasn't an advanced reader, he could make out the question. He carefully searched out the letters on the keyboard in front of him and, using one finger, punched in the letters "J-E-R-K."

"Hi, Jerk," the words on the screen responded cheerily. The crowd snickered. The screen continued to scroll down. "Are you ready to make something delicious to eat?" Adam didn't look at the words long enough to read them but he spied the words at the bottom that commanded him to press "Y" for yes and "N" for no. He pressed "Y." A list of recipes appeared. He picked one at random. I read the words *Chicken Cacciatore* over his head.

"Okay, Jerk, I'm going to tell you how to make Chicken Cacciatore," said the words on the screen. "How many people are you going to feed?" This time Adam read the screen slowly, taking in every word. Then, looking over the numbers at the top of the keyboard, he carefully picked a "one" and then punched in six zeros after it.

The computer never batted an eye or paused to gasp. It immediately went on to say, "Okay, Jerk, take 250,000 chickens, wash and cut them up." The crowd around the computer roared with laughter. The directions continued, oblivious of the reaction. "Then take 500,000 cloves of garlic, finely diced." The directions went on, demanding thousands of gallons of olive oil, millions of pinches of spices—you get the picture.

I finally left to finish my shopping. Adam was still working on the recipe. Periodically, during the next few minutes, I heard the crowd around the computer laughing. My son had found his niche—and it wasn't cooking for a multitude.

I still marvel at the way Adam walked straight up and started punching keys on that computer. I often wish, when I face something unknown but not dangerous, that I had the confidence he had that day.

I learned a lesson while watching Adam at that computer. I'm always thinking about what I should be teaching my children. I should also consider what my children can teach me.

43

MOM, THE TEACHER

Sometimes I'm a terrible teacher of my own children. Here's an example.

"This is a straw-legged mosquito," my daughter told me. "Hmmmm," I said. "Very interesting..." I added. I took a brief look at the flattened creature in her hand, then wrapped it in a scrap of paper, packed her and it in the car, and took off for the library. Science lesson time.

"We're going to learn more about insects," I announced, nudging her through the doors of the library. I found the section of books on insects. She sat looking through fairy tale picture books. While I looked up mosquitos, she escaped outside to play on the grass. I searched and searched but could find no mosquitos with the name "straw-legged." Finally I found the correct name of the creature she had shown me. Calling her back in, I showed her. I gave her the correct name. "Hmmmm," she said. "Very interesting..." She wandered off to look at the display cases.

I checked out three books, hoping she'd look at them at home when there weren't so many other distractions. She never touched the books. Finally, when the books were due, I brought up the subject again. I suggested she could learn more about mosquitos and other insects, including their proper names.

"Oh," she answered, "I don't care what they are really named—I like to make up my own names. I named that one the straw-legged mosquito because of the stripes on his legs. Remember how it looked?" I didn't. I hadn't paid attention to either the legs or the name she had invented once I found it was "incorrect."

I found the specimen still wrapped in the scrap of paper that was stuck in the pages of one of the books. Indeed, it did have stripes on its legs, just like the old-fashioned drinking straws. "Oh, now I see," I said. "You're a good observer," I added, a little late.

My heart was in the right place but my attention was elsewhere when it had counted. Instead of being sensitive to what my daughter was trying to tell me in the first place, I made a lesson that she wasn't interested in. She didn't care about someone else's classification and labeling scheme of insects—she was more interested in inventing her own. She was being scientific in her observation skills. I should have picked up on that fact. I didn't pay attention because I had my own agenda.

I'm not the only parent who gives lessons children aren't interested in. Remember the story about a toddler in the laundromat who asked a simple question about the change-making machine? The mother took the ball and ran with it, giving a fifteen-minute lesson on math, economics, and how things work. She answered all her own questions. The child was completely uninterested in her lengthy exhortation.

My message is: **pay attention**. What is your child really saying? What is an appropriate response—one that will keep her on her own interest-track? Don't always try to jump her over to yours.

Sensitivity is the name of the game. I wish I had more of it.

_____ **44** _____

SCHOOL SHOES:
SOMETHING TO GET EXCITED ABOUT

My son, Timmy, in June, began to think about the kind of shoes he wanted to buy for school. This was very different from my own experience as a child, when school shoes were nothing to get excited about. In my day, shoes had no style. They tended to be plain and sturdy, made of leather that had to be polished daily. They had no specialization either—except walking. They were good for that and offered plenty of support but no other features. Those shoes lasted forever—probably because they were so ugly. When they finally did wear out, you took them in and got them repaired by a man, who smelled like leather and shoe polish, in a shop full of big sewing machines.

Timmy doesn't even know about these kinds of shoes. The closest he came to finding out was when we rented him a pair of dress shoes for his big brother's wedding.

Times have changed. What kind of shoes to buy is a big decision because they define your worth as a person—at least if you're in the fifth grade. Holes in jeans mean nothing but the name and force rating of your sport shoes mean everything.

After careful consideration, Timmy finally decided on the shoes he wanted. In July, we began the discussion of whether he would get to have these shoes or not. "Does everyone have these fancy sports shoes?" I asked, suspecting they were expensive. He responded with the sad story of a boy destined to start school with plastic no-name tennies that had no air pump features and that weren't even new. He was shocked when I refused to see the child as deprived. He was more shocked when I expressed admiration for both the boy and his parents—the boy for knowing that worth isn't defined by footgear and the parents who, although they have the money, refused to invest it in shoes.

He wasn't convinced. "But, Mom," he protested. "I've just got to have Bo Jackson's." By this point, I was educated enough to know that he was still talking about shoes, though nothing in the name gave me a clue. "How much do they cost?" I asked hesitantly, hoping my suspicions about price were wrong. I was willing to pay $50.00. Maybe they fell in this price range. "About $90.00," came his matter of fact answer. I fainted dead away. When Timmy finally revived me, I managed to whisper—"I'll pay half." That moment was the beginning of a long series of negotiations. We finally reached an agreement involving joint financing the week before school started.

As we left the shoe store, Timmy walked tall and proud on his new cushions of air. We were just getting into the car when he grabbed my arm, excitedly pointing toward a crowd of kids. "Look, Mom!" he said breathlessly. I strained my neck to follow his pointing finger. I couldn't see anything to get excited about. "What?" I asked. "What am I looking at?" "That's my **next** pair of school shoes."

45

WHEN WILL THEY EVER
LEARN TO TIE THEIR SHOES?

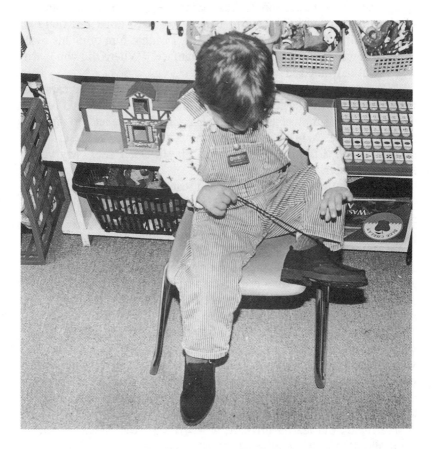

Some children learn the importance
of keeping shoes tied in preschool;
others don't learn until college.

Photo credit: Robert Sturm

You teach and teach your children but sometimes the lesson doesn't come from you. Case in point—shoe-tying.

I remember the agonies of trying to teach my first son, Bruce, to tie his shoes. I started before he had the coordination; anxious, as most parents are that he learn early. He didn't. We sat on the floor together with my talking and his trying to get one end to obey my commands in relationship to the other end. After a number of sessions that ended in both of us crying, we gave up. I just tied his shoes for him. Then one day, much later, I caught him tying his own shoes. He was doing it quietly without fanfare. "Where did you learn that?" I asked, amazed.

"Oh, Aunt Margaret taught me—see, these are two rabbit ears..." He showed me the large loops he had made out of each end of the shoe lace. "And they chase each other round the tree and go right in the hole...here." He demonstrated the actions he was describing, pulled the loops tight, and ran out to play. "Oh, I see." My voice floated out after him.

I did see—I'm just not such a good teacher of my children. Then there's the story of Timmy and his air-augmented sports shoes. He had to have just the right ones—designed to fit and do their job to perfection. A good deal of brain power went into the design of these shoes. Only one factor was left out of the plan that the shoe engineers came up with—kids don't tie their shoes anymore. I don't know if it's an overreaction to velcro or just style. In any case, in spite of the potential for the perfect fit, Timmy's shoes constantly slopped up and down on his feet.

That leads me to Adam. When he graduated from college, I was surprised to see untied shoes protruding from his black gown. He was able to learn all that was required to hold the engineering degree he had in his hand but he still hadn't learned my number one lesson, the one that I had been yelling about since he was a kindergartner—"Tie your shoes!"

He finally did learn—the hard way. (If you read "hee, hee, hee" right about here, it's really not intended.)

The clincher lesson came when Adam fulfilled one of his biggest dreams—parachute jumping. He called me, excited about his accomplishment. He waited until it was over to tell me so he wouldn't worry old mom. He was most anxious to give all the details, even at the long distance rate. "There I was, Mom, first in line—sitting crowded into the back of this little plane that had no doors on it. I was in front of the door facing empty blue sky; my feet sticking out in front. The instructor kept up a steady line of instructions—probably so we wouldn't be nervous. I felt the other guys crammed in around me. We were all ready to jump."

I held my breath, thinking the next line would start a description of the descent. I was wrong. "The guy was just ready to give the command to jump when he looked at my feet," he continued. "'Adam's shoes are untied' he shouted to the crowd in horror. Then he turned to me and he sounded just like you—'Tie your shoes, Adam,' he said."

I swear a smile didn't cross my face as I listened to this story. "I couldn't tie them," Adam continued. "I just couldn't reach my feet with all the stuff on. It was a horrible moment. One of the other guys had to tie my shoes."

The rest of the story is an anticlimax—at least as far as I'm concerned. He jumped; he made it; he loved it. He tested his courage and achieved manhood—or whatever it was he was trying to prove with the jump. But best of all (in my opinion)—he finally learned how important it is to keep his shoes tied.

Also of Interest...
HOW DO I LOVE ME? 2/E
Helen M. Johnson

This excellent book on self-esteem grew out of the author's many years of successfully teaching people of all ages and walks of life how to get a high level of self-esteem *and how to keep it.* Ms. Johnson's experience as an elementary school teacher, high school and college counselor, lecturer, consultant and workshop leader have been drawn upon to develop this readable and practical "How To" book on self-esteem.

Important features:
- Down-to-earth examples
- "Work Outs" in each chapter help facilitate application
- Can be used in a classroom, group, one-on-one, or personally
- Concise and readable
- Action plan puts it all together

105 pages ● paperback ● ISBN 0-88133-224-0

For additional information or to order, please write or call:

Sheffield Publishing Company
P.O. Box 359
Salem, WI 53168
(414) 843-2281